At David C Cook, we equip the local church around
the corner and around the globe to make disciples.
Come see how we are working together—go to
www.davidccook.com. Thank you!

transforming lives together

What people are saying about …

CITY CHANGERS

"Alan Platt is an inspiring, visionary leader who has not just prayed for citywide change … he has led it. Alan has created a movement of unified churches working together for radical city transformation. His journey from concern to compassion will move you to believe God for the miraculous in your city, and this book will give you the tools you need to be a catalyst for change."

J. Todd Mullins, MDiv, senior pastor
of Christ Fellowship Church

"There has never been a more critical time in history for the global church to discern and actuate transformational change in their cities. In this book, my friend and city transformation leader Alan Platt draws from a deep well of experience and shares practical Bible-based wisdom on how to be a twenty-first-century church purveying peace in the midst of the chaos currently dominating and characterizing the city culture."

Rob Hoskins, president of OneHope, Inc.

"I have the privilege of being on Alan Platt's leadership team at Doxa Deo in South Africa, where Alan Platt consistently inspires us to greater depths of understanding and implementing city transformation. This book will help you see God's perspective on the life and purpose of the church in a glorious new way. I highly recommend *City Changers* to every Christian leader so every city and town can see the church rise up to be a light that displays the glory of God in every sphere of society."

Jean Symons, pastor, and leader of
Doxa Deo Team in South Africa

"Alan Platt is one of the most visionary and strategic minds I have met. When a diversified church is unified in purpose and strategy to serve, it brings change to the city. When a unified church strategically mobilizes every member to be a city changer, people will see and experience God in all spheres of society. It is about new churches, reaching new people, that impact our society. Let the voice from the south influence our thinking and action in the north."

Øivind Augland, founder and leader of M4
Europe, convener and networker of NC2P
Europe, and leader of xpand Norway

CITY
CHANGERS

CITY
CHANGERS

*Being the Presence of Christ
in Your Community*

ALAN PLATT

David C Cook®
transforming lives together

CITY CHANGERS
Published by David C Cook
4050 Lee Vance Drive
Colorado Springs, CO 80918 U.S.A.

David C Cook U.K., Kingsway Communications
Eastbourne, East Sussex BN23 6NT, England

The graphic circle C logo is a registered trademark of David C Cook.

LCCN 2017950931
ISBN 978-1-4347-1094-9
eISBN 978-1-4347-1097-0

© 2017 Alan Platt

The Team: Alice Crider, Jeff Gerke, Amy Konyndyk, Abby DeBenedittis, Kayla Fenstermaker, Susan Murdock
Cover Design: Nick Lee
Cover Photo: Pexels

Printed in the United States of America
First Edition 2017

1 2 3 4 5 6 7 8 9 10

103017

CONTENTS

INTRODUCTION

Babylon.

The name is synonymous with corruption and godlessness. The Bible condemns it from Genesis, where the Tower of Babel (another name for Babylon) represents humanity's effort to become God (see Gen. 11), all the way to Revelation, where Babylon is referred to as the mother of prostitutes and abominations of the earth (see Rev. 17:5). There are about three hundred references to Babylon in the Bible, and in many of those, Babylon is portrayed as the antitype—the opposite—of Jerusalem. Babylon was a powerful city, affluent and influential. It was the seat of human power and the symbol of the rejection of God at its greatest height.

Sound familiar?

I am a citizen of the world. I hail from Pretoria, South Africa. My team and I have planted churches across that country and also in London; Stuttgart, Germany; and Auckland, New Zealand—and several more around the world are in preparation stages. Our current global headquarters is in Fort Lauderdale, Florida.

As I have walked the streets and breathed the air of these cities and so many others, I have seen lostness, pain, and brokenness running as rampant as the Bible depicts in ancient Babylon. These cities are affluent and influential, and right alongside human achievement marches human depravity.

I often ask myself whether this narrative can be changed. I wonder what may be done so that this confused generation will discover the grace of God, a gift He shares freely with all humanity.

We live in a world where violence done by people against people is so prevalent, there's not enough time on the news to talk about it all. These days, a murderous rampage has to be spectacular in some way, or extremely close to home, to get coverage on the air.

Children are abducted, raped, and murdered, then dropped into dumpsters. Pregnant women are gunned down while answering the door. Terrorists line up prisoners to decapitate them for the camera or burn them alive in cages. Illegal drag races force other drivers off the road, leaving beloved innocents dead or paralyzed. Drug capos have honest judges assassinated in front of their children. World leaders are deposed for corruption and murder—or worse: they're *not* deposed.

And those are just the news stories I happened to read on the day I wrote this.

Never mind our epidemics of war crimes, genocide, ethnic violence and injustice, child abuse, cronyism, graft, fraud, divorce, drug use, homelessness, dehumanization, elder abuse, and abortion, just to name a few.

If you're like me, you're ready to cry out, "Give us wisdom, understanding, and strategy, Lord Jesus! Help us raise and release city changers who can engage this reality and make a difference."

Stay Awhile

In the Old Testament, the Jewish people had the belief that since God was their God, they were pretty much kings of the world and would always be protected as a nation. When the superpowers of the day came calling, God would surely save them, and there would always be a king in Jerusalem.

Never would the Assyrians prove superior to them. Never would the Egyptians. Never would the Philistines, no matter how many Goliaths they brought with them. And certainly, never, ever, *ever* would the corrupt Babylonians, the most evil regime under the sun, ever prove mightier than the armies of Israel backed by Jehovah, their God.

Except that's exactly what happened.

To the people of Israel, Babylon was everything Jerusalem was not. Babylon was dedicated to false gods, while Jerusalem was dedicated to the one true God. Babylon was the center of pagan worship; Jerusalem hosted the only holy worship. Babylon was characterized by sin, while Jerusalem was the home of those worshippers blessed to live on God's holy hill, where the ark of the covenant resided and where Solomon's temple towered over the city. Jerusalem was God's preferred address on Earth.

Which is why it was an utter shock when Babylon defeated Israel's armies, tore down the walls of Jerusalem, desecrated the temple, and hauled off their leaders and thousands of Jews to live—and die—in exile, nine hundred miles from their home.

As you might imagine, the Jews taken captive to Babylon did not make the transition well. Their entire national identity, not to mention their faith, seemed to have been ripped from them. What they really wanted was for God to instantly judge Babylon and send them home to Jerusalem ASAP.

Imagine them sitting by the Euphrates, where they'd hung their harps on the branches of the willow trees. The Babylonians came to them and said, "We've heard you sing beautiful songs. Won't you sing us a song?" They answered, "How shall we sing the LORD's song in a foreign land?" (Ps. 137:4).

How can we sing any song, much less songs praising God, in this ungodly land? How can we exercise that which is spiritually precious to us here in Babylon, the seat of everything corrupt? To sing those songs, we have to go back to Jerusalem.

On cue, some men among them rose up, claiming to be prophets from God, teaching that God had promised to overthrow their captors and send them home soon.

But the prophet Jeremiah, who had managed to remain in Jerusalem, really did hear from God, and he sent a letter to the exiles. Here's the part that must've been a bitter pill for the displaced Jews to accept:

> Thus says the LORD of hosts, the God of Israel, to all
> the exiles whom I have sent into exile from Jerusalem

to Babylon, "Build houses and live in them; and plant gardens and eat their produce. Take wives and become the fathers of sons and daughters, and take wives for your sons and give your daughters to husbands, that they may bear sons and daughters; and multiply there and do not decrease. *Seek the welfare of the city where I have sent you into exile,* and pray to the LORD on its behalf; *for in its welfare you will have welfare.*" For thus says the LORD of hosts, the God of Israel, "Do not let your prophets who are in your midst and your diviners deceive you, and do not listen to the dreams which they dream. For they prophesy falsely to you in My name; I have not sent them," declares the LORD. (Jer. 29:4–9 NASB)

Did you catch all that? God said He *sent* them into exile. They'd thought it was some sort of fluke or anomaly in the universe, for how else could God have been overpowered by the power of Babylon? No fluke, Jeremiah said. God sent you there. He's doing something intentional. You're there for a reason.

Then he said they were not going to be rescued anytime soon. Those so-called prophets among you saying you're about to come home … don't listen to them. Don't pay attention to their alleged visions and dreams. I haven't told them to say that, because it isn't true. Later in the letter, he said they're going to be in Babylon for *seventy years* (see v. 10).

But just as they were preparing to fight a long campaign of bitterness against their cruel captors, God dropped the A-bomb on them:

Build houses and live in them; and plant gardens and eat their produce. Take wives and become the fathers of sons and daughters, and take wives for your sons and give your daughters to husbands, that they may bear sons and daughters; and multiply there and do not decrease. Seek the welfare of the city where I have sent you into exile, and pray to the LORD on its behalf; for in its welfare you will have welfare. (vv. 5–7 NASB)

Say what? I don't want to build a house here … I want to go home to my real house in Israel. Plant a garden? Never! That implies I'm accepting that this is my reality and will be for the foreseeable future. Marriages and births? Seriously, God, You act as though we're supposed to *like* it here. Are You forgetting how we came to be here? Don't You see their pagan worship? Didn't You see that they dashed our infants against the rock? This place is hateful to us, and You want us to go on as though this is our home now?

And if that weren't enough, God asked them not only to *endure* their captors but also to actively work for—and even *pray* for—their success? *Lord,* I can see them thinking, *I will never pray for the welfare of the ones who defiled Your temple and destroyed Your nation. Never!*

Twenty-First-Century Babylon

A constant cry rises up from the Christians I encounter every day: "Lord, this place is too evil! The people have rejected You and have turned to every kind of evil! Please, won't You rescue us? Could You return today? Or overthrow the evil and install a godly government! You can't mean for us to live *here*."

Now, I'm all for being rescued out of this corrupt world. Who wouldn't want to go from godlessness to the freedom of God's perfect world in a single heartbeat? If that's God's plan, I'm on board with it 100 percent.

However, I'm pretty sure that's not God's plan. At least, not yet. My take on it is that God is saying to us exactly what He said to the exiles:

- Build houses and live in them.
- Plant gardens and eat their produce.
- Take wives and become the fathers of sons and daughters.
- Take wives for your sons and give your daughters to husbands.
- Multiply there and do not decrease.
- Seek the welfare of the city where I have sent you into exile.
- Pray to the Lord on its behalf, for in its welfare you will have welfare.

We're in exile here on this earth. The Bible calls Christians "aliens" and "foreigners" whose true citizenship is above (see 1 Pet. 1:1 NASB; 1 Pet. 2:11 NIV; Phil. 3:20).

Someday He will change it all in the blink of an eye. But until He does, I think He wants us to dig in, settle down, go about our lives, and seek the welfare of the land of our exile. Because our welfare is found in the welfare of this place.

Did you know that Jeremiah 29:11, that famous verse about how God will make everything turn out all right for you in the end, comes from this same letter of Jeremiah to the exiles?

> For thus says the LORD, "When seventy years have been completed for Babylon, I will visit you and fulfill My good word to you, to bring you back to this place. For I know the plans that I have for you," declares the LORD, "plans for welfare and not for calamity to give you a future and a hope. Then you will call upon Me and come and pray to Me, and I will listen to you. You will seek Me and find Me when you search for Me with all your heart. I will be found by you," declares the LORD, "and I will restore your fortunes and will gather you from all the nations and from all the places where I have driven you," declares the LORD, "and I will bring you back to the place from where I sent you into exile." (Jer. 29:10–14 NASB)

I think that verse, sometimes used by Christians in a bumper sticker sort of way, has deeper impact when we remember it's being used to tell heartbroken believers that they're going to be stuck in their torment for many, many more years but that God has not forgotten them.

May that lift our hearts as well. Because God is asking not that we hunker down here to endure without a vision of the perfect future that awaits us but that we actively seek the good of the Babylon of our own exile.

The Good of Our Babylon

We must allow this truth to change our way of thinking. We need to understand the kingdom mind-set that takes us beyond wanting to escape the world and challenges us to immerse ourselves in it.

God has a plan for our own Babylon. The communities and cities where we live are on God's agenda, and we, His people, are the agents that could bring *shalom* (peace and wholeness) into those environments. Because now we, His children, are God's preferred address on Earth. We are the peace of God that can be for the wholeness of the earth.

God is clearly doing something wonderful in our day, and transformed communities are a part of this story. When the kingdom of God truly comes to a city, no institution or sector is left unaffected.

That cities around the world are affected by evil is undeniable. What many Christians find difficult to imagine is that the situation could be any other way. Can you picture your city, or your nation, dominated by good? Take a moment to visualize it.

God places us as the carriers of shalom in these broken environments. Evil is not stronger than good. Darkness is not stronger than light. The way things are isn't how they should stay.

City Changers

I have found as I've delivered this message around the world that as soon as I have people envision a city suffused with God's goodness, they immediately have this defeating thought: *But the task is so large—what can I possibly do to make a difference?*

That's where this book comes in!

We need to become city changers. Not alone, but together. God has called us to go beyond personal growth and even church growth in our Christian lives and settle for nothing short of affecting our communities with the shalom of God.

His plan to affect culture is through the church, the body of Christ around the world. But we've had the wrong understanding of so many things for so many years that we're not doing what we should, and as a result, we are losing our cities and watching them become centers of deprivation and environments of lostness, pain, brokenness, and empty pursuits. I'm convinced that God sees cities as a context where life can flourish, and His instrument to bring this to pass is the church.

Our cities are at great risk, and the church can and must step up to meet the challenge. Aligning ourselves with what we believe to be the mission of God, we must begin to close the gap between the current reality and God's vision for our cities. A vision of wholeness in every sphere of society. Because of the urgency of the moment and the opportunity before us, the church must rise to the challenge to do what it does in a fresh and new way.

We have to change our philosophy of ministry. We have to start thinking differently about church, and we will have to start thinking differently about the people who make up the church. We must realize that God wants to do something *through* the people. People are not just coming to church to be *blessed*; they are coming to church to be *equipped*. They are coming to be equipped as city changers. Full-fledged disciples, who will execute God's agenda on the planet. They are not just attending a program—they are the program!

The Vision

God is challenging us with a vision of what our communities—and, indeed, our world—will be like when city changers through whom God does His work roam the land. The vision is aligned with what we read in the book of Isaiah:

> And I, because of what they have planned and done, am about to come and gather the people of all nations and languages, and *they will come and see my glory.*
>
> I will set a sign among them, and I will send some of those who survive to the nations—to Tarshish, to the Libyans and Lydians (famous as archers), to Tubal and Greece, and to the distant islands that have not heard of my fame or seen my glory. *They will proclaim my glory among the nations.* (Isa. 66:18–19 NIV)

This is the vision I have for communities and cities:

- *I see* in my spirit thousands of people across the cities of the world bowing their hearts in surrender before the lordship of Jesus Christ, welcoming His authority and rule in their lives.

- *I see* thousands of people gathering in celebrations across the cities with their hands raised, worshipping Jesus as Lord, and then engaging their world with the knowledge of being called to be the presence of Christ in their communities.

- *I see* the restoration of families and homes as brokenness and pain is healed by the power of love flowing between husbands and wives and children and parents.

- *I see* dads and sons playing together in parks enjoying one another's company and moms and daughters laughing together and enjoying the good things of life. I see children being equipped for life and being trained in a Christ-centered worldview to grow and develop to take their places in society as contributors to the common good.

- *I see* single parents who have struggled to survive being embraced in circles of love and feeling safe through the support and love of God's people as they share resources and God's grace freely.

- *I see* children going to school with excitement, feeling accepted and loved, and receiving quality education.

- *I see* artists who can give expression through creativity redeeming the arts to inspire us, elevate our appreciation, and bring praise to God.
- *I see* businesspeople who excel in building the economy and creating jobs and who are excited to give of their time, gifts, and resources in service of others and the kingdom of God.
- *I see* small groups of people reaching out to one another, supporting people who are going through tough times, investing in their lives the Word and the wisdom of God; I see people meeting on a regular basis in accountability relationships, assisting one another to live in victory, overcoming the challenges that life brings.
- *I see* people reaching out across cultural and racial boundaries to touch lives and share life with one another, to create a society free from prejudice and self-centeredness.
- *I see* churches reaching out to one another, with church leaders embracing one another and standing together to make a difference in every city.
- *I see* sportsmen who live with exemplary character, who fearlessly share their testimonies, raising up a generation who are proud to be followers of Christ.
- *I see* the media publishing that which is true and unbiased, sharing and proclaiming good news and testimonies of the grace of God.

- *I see* cities filled with the presence of Jesus Christ!

This, my friend, is the culture we could live in. I have seen elements of it already. It is what will happen as you, I, and others become city changers.

The Lay of the Land

In order to go from fearing Babylon to affecting and ultimately transforming it, we need to make a series of changes and adopt new strategies. That is what we will focus on in this book.

We have to change our mentality, our theology, our philosophy, and our understanding of the world in order to go beyond simply caring about the condition of our world and begin having active compassion for it. It all begins with understanding who we—you and I—are in God's eyes.

We need a strategy for how to go about affecting the prevailing culture. We need to understand the effect, the presence, the church brings to a community: a fathering presence, a faithful presence, and a fruitful presence.

The immense principle of generosity and what it has to do with the global unity movement we're seeing across the church universal is key to our engagement.

All this leads us to discover the keys to reaching the unreached spaces of our communities for Christ.

Plant a Garden

We've been so conditioned to think of this earth as Satan's that we've surrendered ground that should've been ours the whole time.

If the culture around you is hateful toward your faith, then of course you're going to want to leave it. Good riddance! If you see the world as wholly evil and closing in around you like a dark tide rising, you're certainly going to want to retreat.

But if you see yourself as a purveyor of a miracle medicine, of salvation itself for everyone you meet, suddenly you're not a hunted and surrounded refugee but a powerful rescuer and bringer of light.

Christ didn't send you here to this land to leave it early or simply hide your light behind dark curtains. He sent you here to stay and be His force of transformation in a dark and dying world.

So unpack your bags, build a house here, and plant a garden. New life is about to spring forth from you for the healing of the nations. Even for those in Babylon.

1

FROM CONCERN TO COMPASSION

Our world is not a comfortable place in which to be a Christian today. The globe has seemingly gone crazy, and there is an ever-increasing sense that darkness is soon to prevail—or may already be prevailing—in so many areas of society. We are caught up in a cultural reality where conflict and controversy have become the order of the day. For most Christians, the world has become a challenging reality, and we need God's wisdom and power to navigate and thrive in the midst of its Babylonian nature.

Political power plays, economic instability, pride, and personal gain at the expense of others seem to define our culture. Mainstream media is no longer a trusted source of answers, so social media steps in, peddling volumes of confusion and in its own way making the world even more dangerous.

It seems such a long way from what we would wish. We all want to live in communities that are blessed, functional spaces where we can truly flourish. We want to live in neighborhoods that are safe and free of discrimination. We want our schools to be places where real learning happens. We want our justice system to serve everyone fairly. We want economic opportunity for citizens of every class and ethnicity. We desire that the arts and media be redeemed from celebrating depravity so they can again be a voice of hope, restoration, and prophetic insight. We desire leaders who engender trust, create an environment of faith through good governance, and live lives of integrity.

Most of all, we want people to hear and respond to the call to enjoy seamless relationship with God as they commit their lives to the lordship of Jesus Christ.

We all want communities like that. I want to live in a community like that!

Salt and Light

I used to believe that such a thing was impossible, that the influence of evil was too powerful to resist, and that we had to hunker down and hold on until the end of our days. I don't think that anymore. Now I know the goodness of the Lord can prevail on Earth, and I know it will come through a life-giving church.

As Christians, we often do not realize that we have a fundamental contribution to make to ensure the quality of our communities. Where we do the things we should, our cities are deeply affected and transformed. Where we fail to do those things, our cities continue to sink into darkness.

In essence, the church deserves the communities it has.

There is a mandate on us as God's people to engage communities in such a way that we will see His glory manifested in every sphere of society. Many cities are suffering because of a scarcity of Christian presence. In those places, the church isn't a base for transforming culture but a bomb shelter against it. We withdraw and throw up walls, and because of our absence, communities have been orphaned from our life-giving engagement. To embrace God's mission is to offer our communities the love, wisdom, respect, and service they so desperately need.

We are bombarded with information that seems to say the world has sunk too far to be saved. No wonder we just want to withdraw and find a safe place to wait it out.

But these evil times, however uncomfortable they may be to us, have not caught God by surprise. He is not watching from a distance, some passive and detached celestial being mildly interested in how we walk through our years. The Lord God is dynamically active in our world, and His plan is to empower us as His agents of grace with one audacious idea: that ordinary people can be used to change the world for good. That we can be city changers, and thus world changers.

To set the stage for your own shift from concern to compassion, I need to tell you my own story.

How I Became a City Changer

My journey began many years ago when I was a young church leader in the middle of a massive political transition in South Africa.

Our ministry started in Pretoria, South Africa, about a quarter of a century ago, and since then we have been on the journey of reaching communities and engaging culture. Now, all this time later, we are sharing our experiences and seeing God move on every continent.

In 1992, my wife and I took over a church that had gone through a major crisis. This church had incredible promise, and it had a beautiful building that could seat one thousand people. But most of those seats were empty. The church had suffered through a number of leadership disappointments, and there were only about 350 people left in the church. According to South African standards, where churches tend to run large, that officially made it a small church. The church was in deep debt, and the people were in a state of serious confusion.

We knew we needed God to help us. But for some reason, I had the sense that God wanted to do something amazing through this church, not only within its walls but far beyond them.

I was thirty-two at the time, and my only leadership experience was as a youth pastor at my previous church. The former leaders at this new church had all been well known and well qualified—they all had doctoral degrees—and who was I? I felt like a David who had come from nowhere, yet suddenly I had this responsibility.

But what I came to learn was that when God has a plan, He fulfills His purposes ... if He can find a man or a woman prepared to trust Him. If one generation does not take hold of the inheritance, God raises another generation to do so. An entire generation taking up His cause can begin with one person taking up His cause. So I made the decision that it would be me. "Lord," I said, "I want the inheritance in my generation."

Within two years after we started ministering at that church, a miracle took place. About thirteen hundred people joined the church. Once again, even by South African standards, that is amazing momentum. People were coming to the church, and the city was talking about us, and we were excited.

Two years into that journey (in 1994), I was sitting in my study preparing for a leadership meeting one evening. I opened the Bible, and it fell to 1 Corinthians 12, where Paul speaks about spiritual gifts. Of course, I knew that passage very well, but as I was reading it that time, one portion suddenly stood out: "To one is given ... faith by the same Spirit" (vv. 8–9).

As I read those words, I felt as if the Bible were now reading *me*. I had a profound sense of the presence of God in my study, and I had the impression that God was speaking these words directly to me. It seemed He said, "Remember how, when you came here two years ago, many people did not believe this church would rise again, much less become an influence in this city? And do you remember that you did believe it?"

By that time, I was crying. "Yes, Lord," I said. "It's true—I believed it."

What God impressed on me so clearly was that it was not my own faith that had brought me to believe that the miraculous growth and influence of the church would happen but it was a gift of faith from Him. He'd given me the faith to believe it. *To one is given the gift of faith.*

For the first time in my life, I became aware that I had been functioning under the empowerment of the Holy Spirit to believe in something that I naturally would not be able to.

I later came to understand that many times in our lives the Holy Spirit empowers us with faith or wisdom or knowledge or power, though we are unaware of it. Perhaps you can recall moments in your life when you felt led to believe in something even though that was not the posture you would normally take.

But it was the next part of that conversation with God that changed my life. He'd already told me He was the one who'd given me the faith to believe the church could grow exponentially. Now I sensed the Holy Spirit impressing this on my heart: *"I now give you the faith to trust Me for a city!"*

I don't know how to explain it, except to say that in that moment I became pregnant with conviction that a whole city, an entire geographical region, could come under the dominant influence of the presence of Jesus Christ.

Telling the Elder Board

At the conclusion of that incredible time with God, I wrote down two notes I felt burning in me:

- *Faith for a church*
- *Faith for a city*

I went to the leadership meeting that evening aware that God had spoken to me but uncertain how to verbalize the experience. There were people on the team who were extremely mature both in life and in their spiritual journeys. They would be evaluating my communication through the lens of years of experience in church leadership. They had been through difficult times, thanks to their previous leaders, and the last thing they needed was an overexcited young pastor with a "new vision" that he had been called to change the world.

The meeting began, and I felt God telling me I shouldn't say much. We sang together in worship and then entered a time of silent reflection. After some minutes, one of the senior leaders indicated that he sensed he'd received a word from God to share with us. He lifted his chin and in a clear voice said, "God says He is calling us to embrace the city."

I couldn't believe it. Had God spoken to this man too? I wanted to share my own experience right then, but I again felt I should stay on my knees and keep quiet.

One by one the leaders shared that their hearts were confirming this as a conviction and a message from God. The fascinating thing about all this was that it wasn't as if we'd spent previous meetings talking about reaching out to the city. Actually, before then we had never communicated about the city as a focus of the church. We had spoken at length in our previous gatherings about being a healthy church, a growing church, and a discipling church, but we'd never talked about us as a church that had been called to engage the city. And yet here was the entire leadership team saying that God was redirecting us.

It was then that I took my notes and read them to the leaders. "My friends, God spoke to me in my study just before I came here. I wrote down only two things from that encounter, things I knew I must share with you tonight. I wrote 'Faith for a church' and 'Faith for a city.' I believe God has given us the gift of faith to believe Him for our entire city."

As we dialogued about what this new vision would mean, we realized God was not saying He wanted us to take over the city in the sense of controlling areas of the city with a political agenda. We wanted to be sure we did not confuse the call to *engage* our community with an attitude of dominion or triumphalism.

We were also very aware that God was not saying everybody in the city would join our church. We knew we were on a growth trajectory that would likely continue until we were a large church in our city, although that had never been our focus. We were not to feel we were God's only agency in the city, but rather, we were to engage it with service, wisdom, and the power of the Holy Spirit.

We left that meeting knowing God had spoken. But we also knew we had no idea where to start. How do you serve, affect, and change a city? We can dialogue about it philosophically, and we can preach about it, but how do we actually start? I knew we needed wisdom. For the next two years, every time we came together as a leadership team, we would pray for wisdom, understanding, and strategy. Our prayer many times was "Lord, You told us to do this, and we don't want to start just another program. We want to understand how You want us to do this."

As time went on, we began to feel God giving us a strategy. We felt so strongly that this was God's identity for our church that, after two years and when we thought we understood it, we relaunched our church with a new name: Doxa Deo.

The name was inspired by this verse:

> For the earth will be filled
> With the knowledge of the glory of the LORD,
> As the waters cover the sea. (Hab. 2:14)

We combined the Greek word for *glory* (*doxa*) with the Latin word for *God* (*Deo*). Doxa Deo—the *glory of God* revealed in our city.

Expanding the Vision

We are now extremely engaged in Pretoria, and we have a distinct influence in various areas of the city. Over the years, God has also blessed us so that the church has kept growing. At the time of this writing, we gather in fourteen campuses or sites across the city, where we currently serve thirty thousand people. These different campuses form one church in the city. We don't use technology to cause all the sites to see the same message at the same time. Rather, we focus on raising leaders at each campus, both to lead and to communicate.

Ten years into our love embrace of Pretoria, we sensed the challenge to establish Doxa Deo in twelve cities across the world.

We realized early on that no matter how big we grew, Doxa Deo Church could not do this all by itself. So we worked hard to bring other churches into the dialogue. We knew we needed to get the church to come together in unity of fellowship and action. As fellow believers, we felt *our* city was *our* responsibility.

This book was envisioned to be an instrument of challenge and empowerment to people who want to make a difference in this world. My prayer is that it will be useful to every Christ follower as well as to leaders in both the church and marketplace environments.

Five Guiding Principles

Where do you begin if you want to touch a city? When I started speaking to people about transforming the city, I saw that kind of blur in their eyes.

"The city? Like the whole, entire city? Do you have an idea how big this city is? Can we really touch and affect a city? Where would we even start?"

Right away, we knew we needed a plan of action. We prayed that God would give us clear strategy. We sensed God prompting us in various ways, but one of the clearest was the story from Mark 6 about Jesus feeding the five thousand. In it, we discovered five principles that became guiding lights for our journey. These principles are transferable to any community, no matter how big or small or how poor or rich that community might be.

- Change your mentality—move from concern to compassion
- Develop a strategy—prepare for the miracle
- Take small steps—start by breaking off small pieces
- Multiply the impact—release others and form strategic partnerships
- Engage the other side—find the keys to unreached people and spaces

The first principle we learned was that we needed to *change our mentality.* We needed a new way of thinking. This new mentality was made evident in the difference between the disciples and Jesus. In that story, you will recall that the disciples had *concern* for the hungry people, but that's as far as it went. They saw the problem. They were aware of the looming challenge. But it says Jesus had *compassion.*

The disciples showed their concern by coming to Jesus and saying, "Let's send the people away so they can get food." As soon as they saw the problem, they became aware that they didn't have the resources to deal with it. They felt helpless and said, "What difference can we make?"

They were concerned but not engaged. Concern does not necessarily take responsibility. Concern sees the problem but is hamstrung by the lack of resources to effectively make a difference. So concern wants to send the problem away, hoping that someone else, somehow, will take care of it.

For years, the church has been an institution of concern only. We're concerned about our communities. We are concerned about the brokenness, the pain, the lostness, the things that are negative within our world. We love to quote statistics. We explain and condemn things around us. We even rant and rave from pulpits about how bad things are and how broken and sinful society is. We address those things with eloquence and zeal.

But we don't always get involved. We often don't move from *concern* to *compassion*.

Jesus rejected the disciples' well-meaning but insufficient plan for how to deal with the hungry crowd. Jesus told them *they* were going to give the people something to eat. Jesus was not intimidated by the obvious lack of resources.

You see, concern sends people away and hopes that someone else will address the problem. Compassion rolls up its sleeves and gets involved. Compassion starts making a difference.

Many times we're like the disciples. We're *concerned* about so many things. We preach about our concerns, discuss our concerns, and inform the Lord in prayer about our concerns—and then we hope somebody else will take care of them. We found ourselves confronted by this question: How can we move from the mentality of the disciples to the mentality of Jesus? How can we move from concern to compassion?

A Threefold Conversion

This change requires a "whole gospel" understanding of engagement, which we can see illustrated in the story of the Old Testament prophet Micah.

Micah was called by God to speak His words to Jerusalem. He spoke not as a city dweller but as a peasant from a rural area. In Jerusalem, other peasants were exploited. They were seen to be worthy to make money for the city but not worthy to share in the profits of their own labors. Jerusalem, the city of God, was full of corruption, abuse, and leaders dedicated to selfish gain, a city filled with brokenness and pain.

It is within this context that Micah cries out to God, and in chapter 6, we see God's reply. He calls the city and the leaders to account for their lies. It is as if God opens a court case against the city and outlines the things that are important to Him:

> He has shown you, O man, what is good;
> And what does the LORD require of you
> But to do justly,
> To love mercy,
> And to walk humbly with your God? (Mic. 6:8)

Do justly, love mercy, and walk humbly with God. Some commentators call this a threefold conversion that every Christian needs to have.

First, of course, is our conversion to God. That's when we come to Christ in faith and experience the privilege of discovering our inclusion in the accomplished work of Christ.

Second, we need to have the conversion to living beyond ourselves, to serving others.

And third is a conversion to the public, social, and political arenas.

The Doxa Deo model, and the model I'm outlining in this book, embraces all three dimensions as the framework of everything we do. We have defined them as follows:

- Knowing God ("walk humbly with your God")
- Loving people ("love mercy")
- Impacting your world ("do justly")

If we want to be engaged sustainably in our communities, we have to understand these three dimensions. For that reason, our preaching, teaching, equipping, and disciple making center around these three focus areas.

At Doxa Deo, that means we affectionately speak about *raising city changers* as our primary focus and fundamental ministry. Our discipleship framework starts with the children's ministry curriculum, our youth training program, and the messages from the pulpit. Everything else we do to train and equip our people centers around strengthening these three basic outcomes, resulting in city changers, not members only.

We have become serious about equipping people who spend most of their time in Babylon. These brave believers need to be empowered to function in the challenging environment of this world.

So I run straight to the goal with purpose in every
step. I fight to win. I'm not just shadow-boxing or
playing around. (1 Cor. 9:26 TLB)

If our cities are to be transformed, it will happen through transformed people. As a rule, churches don't produce city changers. Many
produce just attending church members. The quality and intensity of
our discipleship processes must change. History gives endorsement
to the fact that all transformation in the world happens when people
become convinced that what they believe is what the world needs.

It's an inside-out strategy: the church, which is already inside a
culture, works outward to transform that culture. Jesus focused on
just this strategy. It began with the radical transformation of a small
group of people called the disciples. In a very short span of time, they
filled Jerusalem with their teaching (see Acts 5:28) and "the number
of disciples in Jerusalem increased rapidly" (Acts 6:7 NIV).

With a growing number of Christ's disciples, the city of
Jerusalem would never be the same. These people did not, however,
make these changes while sitting comfortably in a safe space called a
church building.

It was risky at times and carried a good measure of persecution,
but somehow they counted it a privilege even to suffer while representing what they believed.

So they departed from the presence of the council,
rejoicing that they were counted worthy to suffer
shame for His name. And daily in the temple, and

in every house, they did not cease teaching and
preaching Jesus as the Christ. (Acts 5:41–42)

If you want to be a city changer, beware! I am definitely not
promising that this will be compatible with the comfortable Christian
culture we find today. Rather, it's a call to radical engagement that
might position you in service, or even in sacrifice, at a level beyond
what Christians today have ever known. This would come as a special shock to those who might have embraced Christ thinking they
would thereby get a more comfortable life.

I'm not saying you're signing up for martyrdom. But I am calling
you to align yourself with the mission of God.

In Doxa Deo, we do not speak about people becoming *members*.
We refer to them as *partners*. We don't want members, but we do want
partners in the dream. Those who join with us become colaborers
who sign up to share the burden of believing that our communities
can be radically transformed.

We desperately need a return to the inside-out approach of Jesus.
That is, transformation begins by knowing God, loving people, and
influencing the society around you. Many in our day profess to be
Christians, but there is a woeful lack of transformed disciples who
can represent the kingdom life necessary to produce true societal and
community transformation.

2

THE ACCOMPLISHED WORK OF CHRIST

If our cities are to be transformed, it will happen through transformed people. It saddens me when I speak with Christians who do not understand who they actually are in Christ. If we want to see communities change, it must start with people discovering who they truly are in Christ and learning how to represent this new life in broken communities. If Christ followers have the wrong understanding of who they are, they will not have the influence to affect society. They are children of light, no longer subject to the dominion of darkness, yet many live as if nothing has changed.

We are now in Christ, and Christ is in us. Until we all understand that and live in it fully, it will always be beyond our reach to become city changers who can bring about the kind of community and culture we long to live in. Meaningful change in our culture, and enduring change in communities, is rooted in *transformed character*.

This kind of change begins in the lives of individuals who have been transformed into the image of the Son of God.

True transformation in communities will be sustained only when we establish people in their true identity, revealed through the redemption in Jesus Christ. We need gospel-centered environments that will create an understanding of God's intention for their individual lives and their effect on society. All true transformation starts with and is sustained by *knowing God.*

Knowing God means gaining a deep understanding of God's work in the three dimensions of *identification, intimacy,* and *integrity.*

Identification

The gospel is *good news.* It is the good news that you and I were included in the redemption purchased by Jesus Christ on the cross. You were fully implicated in the fall of Adam. You became a sinner—not because you sinned but because you were included in the bloodline of Adam.

In the same way, you were fully included in the redemption won by Jesus. You have been proclaimed righteous, not because of your own righteous deeds but because you were folded into the moment of His perfect sacrifice and victory on the cross. Through faith in Christ's completed work on the cross, you and I no longer approach life from the perspective of the fall of Adam but from the perspective of victory in Christ.

That bears repeating: You are no longer living in Adam— defeated, declared guilty, full of sin, awaiting punishment. You are now living in Christ—victorious, declared innocent, full of God's righteousness, and forever beyond punishment.

Living in light of Jesus's completed work is a daily choice. Every minute, you can choose to live from the Tree of Life (the victory of Christ on our behalf) or from the Tree of Knowledge of Good and Evil (continuing to practice the inferior life in Adam).

A New Paradigm

It will help to look at how Paul discussed this in the book of Romans:

> For all have sinned and fall short of the glory of God, being justified freely by His grace through the redemption that is in Christ Jesus. (Rom. 3:23–24)

The first part (v. 23) is the bad news, the old truth: everyone stood condemned before God because everyone had sinned, both directly and through the bloodline of Adam. Then comes the very, very good news (v. 24): we now stand justified—not because of anything we'd done but because of Christ's completed work.

All ministry done right originates from verse 24, not verse 23.

So many Christians are still trying to fix themselves, as if they're stuck in verse 23. They talk about their sinfulness, their tendency to rebel against God, and their unworthiness. I think they may do it partially out of a well-intentioned desire to remain humble before God and not think too highly of themselves in relation to Him. But what it results in is a false humility and a defeated life, so far from what God intended for them as to be almost unrecognizable.

When a godly couple adopts a child, they don't want that child to grow up saying, "I'm so sorry I'm not really your child. I won't eat much, I promise. I won't make a mess or make any sounds or ask anything of you. I'm so, so sorry that my existence causes you to have to buy more groceries. If you have any awful jobs, please give them to me. Nothing is too degrading for me—it's only what I deserve. I vow to dedicate my life to trying to make you not sorry you took me in."

Of course not! That couple wants the child to forget all about being adopted and wants him or her to feel exactly like a child naturally born into the family. They want the child to make noise and make messes and raid the fridge and put things on the grocery list and act entirely as if he or she fully and permanently belongs. They want the child to live in joy and security and to exercise all the privileges of being a beloved part of the family.

So many Christians live as though God must be sorry He let them into His family. Maybe they stowed away or got there illegitimately. Maybe they bribed the butler and sneaked in unawares. They try to live so that God won't notice them and remember how He really does need to kick them out once and for all.

But God wants His children to live as though they own the place. He wants them to live like royalty. Not in the sense of bossing people around or behaving arrogantly, but in the sense of taking authority and living as if they really do belong in the castle.

Everything we do as Christians—our preaching, teaching, counseling, evangelism, prayers, and worship—must come from understanding that justification has been established in our lives and that we have redemption in Christ Jesus. We are not still negotiating redemption with God, hoping to win His favor someday. No, God took the initiative to redeem us. Now it is something we discover more and more through revelation and embrace by faith.

Over the last few years, I have witnessed the rise of what I consider a wonderful practice in the church, and that is what I will refer to as the "come as you are" invitation to all. This means that we in the church will embrace, without any judgment, any person who wants to come to any of our gatherings. However, a common failing I often see in connection with that is the belief that those people should "leave as they were."

Yes, everyone can come to Christ just as they are. The invitation is wide open to all, and no one has to get fixed before coming to the Fixer. But that doesn't mean there should be no revelation that would reposition that person's life. Being accepted in love is the first step. But letting people depart without helping them find fullness of life would not be in line with Christ's redemptive work on the cross.

People who have engaged Jesus and embraced redemption should experience fundamental transformation in their lives. Jesus's followers should all discover the mirror image of their new identity. This identity is being reflected to us through Jesus Christ. For this is what it means to be His disciples.

It is problematic when we as Christ followers, wanting to make people feel comfortable and not judged, portray ourselves as still being "sinners." We somehow forget that some of the worst sinners in the time of Jesus felt very comfortable around Him, though He was the most holy person on the planet. We must be cautious not to degrade the implications of redemption in our effort to create an environment where sinful people feel comfortable. Remember, we are not sinners because we do sinful deeds; we were declared sinners because of our association with Adam. Just as we are not righteous because we do righteous deeds—we are now righteous because we are in Christ.

Divine Exchange

The basis of our new life in Christ is established in the divine exchange that took place on the cross.

> For if by the one man's offense death reigned through the one, much more those who receive abundance of grace and of the gift of righteousness will reign in life through the One, Jesus Christ. (Rom. 5:17)

Adam's sin was applied to all humans. Equally, Jesus's righteousness is offered to all humans too.

Paul goes on:

> Therefore, as through one man's offense judgment came to all men, resulting in condemnation, even so through one Man's righteous act the free gift came to all men, resulting in justification of life. (Rom. 5:18)

In the mystery of God's love plan, one man would die for all people. Spiritually speaking, all people simultaneously died in

Christ's death so that all could legally share in His glory. At the cross, God allowed all people to be represented in the single act of one man's sacrifice, a sacrifice that invalidated the claims of darkness and ignorance over all. When history recorded the death of one man, eternity recorded the repositioning of humanity.

Now, being in Christ, we are no longer sinners—we are the very righteousness of God:

> For He made Him who knew no sin to be sin for
> us, *that we might become the righteousness of God* in
> Him. (2 Cor. 5:21)

We may still choose to sin, but that's not the same as being sinners. That was our condition when we were still in Adam, before we came to Christ. "Sinner" was what defined us, even when we sometimes miraculously chose not to sin. But now, in Christ, we are redeemed ones—the righteousness of God—and that remains the definition of our character, even when we sometimes choose to sin.

Jesus Christ has paid the price for every human being to be reunited in relationship with God. Scripture is clear that even when we were hostile enemies of God, He reconciled to us to Himself through His Son.

> For if when we were enemies we were reconciled
> to God through the death of His Son, much more,
> having been reconciled, we shall be saved by His
> life. (Rom. 5:10)

So many billions of people on Earth do not understand this. All Christ followers must discover that they have been associated with Christ's death, resurrection, and ascension.

A New Identity

Before Christ came to Earth, God and humanity were separated. In the previous "dispensation" of the Old Testament, when God did speak to mankind, He did so through the prophets. However, when Christ came (in the "new dispensation" recorded in the New Testament), God spoke to mankind through His Son. God opened a new conversation with humanity, and that new conversation now defines our identity and relationship with Him.

> God, who at various times and in various ways
> spoke in time past to the fathers by the prophets,
> has in these last days spoken to us by His Son.
> (Heb. 1:1–2)

God could not speak to humanity with greater clarity or accuracy than He revealed in His Son. If you want to truly understand your place in the universe, you must discover the Son of God, Jesus Christ, because in Him you find your identity and design.

> For those God foreknew he also predestined to be
> conformed to the image of his Son, that he might
> be the firstborn among many brothers and sisters.
> (Rom. 8:29 NIV)

Jesus has become the pattern for our new identity! The essence of the gospel is the knowledge that we have been redeemed to a new creation that finds its design in Him. Our life mission now is to be like Jesus. This is the essence of all discipleship.

Now We Live It Out

Our Author's signature is nowhere better displayed than in our redeemed lives. God has done the work of reconciling us to Him, through Christ.

> But we all, with unveiled face, beholding as in a mirror the glory of the Lord, are being transformed into the same image from glory to glory, just as by the Spirit of the Lord. (2 Cor. 3:18)

The mirror reflects who we are in Christ. This realization is so much more effective than the exercise of our willpower. Our job is to look at a reflection. A mirror shows you only what is real. We must discover who we are now, because we are in Him.

The Greek word behind the English word *glory* in that passage is where we see God's opinion of you and me. The Greek word *doxa* is said to be a word denoting someone's opinion of something. *Vine's Expository Dictionary* defines the word this way: *doxa* "primarily signifies an opinion, estimate, and hence, the honour resulting from a good opinion."[2]

So if we say something is glorious, we're saying we have such a good opinion of it that we praise it. We could call it the "very high opinion resulting in praise." Now let's replace *glory* with that definition in the verse:

> But we all, with unveiled face, beholding as in a
> mirror the *very high opinion resulting in praise* of the
> Lord, are being transformed into the same image
> from *very high opinion resulting in praise* to *very high
> opinion resulting in praise,* just as by the Spirit of
> the Lord.

That is the point of the gospel. And Paul says we can see ourselves in the picture when we behold the glory of God. As we behold Him, we are now discovering, as in a mirror, His opinion of us. We discover who we truly are so we can live as He desires us to live.

Through my beholding Him accurately as in a mirror, I am looking at the proclamation of God over my life. I see Jesus now as the definition of who I am and of who I am becoming. Not in a religious way or getting all sentimental about Him, but in the sense of desiring to know Him more so that I can discover who He has redeemed me to be.

Redemption in our lives happens when we discover ourselves in this good news story and when we judge ourselves as being included in the completed work of Jesus Christ.

> For the love of Christ compels us, because we judge
> thus: that if One died for all, then all died....

> Therefore, from now on, we regard no one
> according to the flesh. Even though we have known

Christ according to the flesh, yet now we know Him
thus no longer. Therefore, if anyone is in Christ, he is
a new creation; old things have passed away; behold,
all things have become new. (2 Cor. 5:14, 16–17)

Our identification with Christ—with His death, His resurrection, and His ascension—is the basis of our new identity. See yourself as dead to your old life, raised into resurrection life, and seated with Him in a position of authority in heavenly places. The impact of the gospel is a transformed life. Not just blessed people or encouraged people, but transformed people.

This newfound sense of being accepted by God also leads the way for us to have liberty to stand in an intimate and quality relationship with the Father.

Intimacy

God is not still making up His mind about humanity. That's already done. Nor am I still negotiating my salvation with God. It's settled. But what is left to do is to discover myself in the initiative of God. I must get back to the reality that God found us in Christ long before He lost us in Adam.

Here's a secret most people have never learned: the primary reward of Christianity is not heaven—the primary reward of Christianity is restored intimacy with the Father. It is only from the perspective of His eternal purpose that we see the true meaning of our lives.

This was evident in the life of Jesus, who was so different from every other human being on the planet.

- There was something unique in how He spoke (as one with authority).
- There was something unique in how He prayed (as if He were personally speaking to the Father).
- There was something unique in how He handled challenges (as if He were aware that He had divine authority).
- There was something unique in how He engaged people (He was not intimidated by their status or sinfulness).

It was clear that Jesus lived with a deep awareness of the presence of the Father in His life. He said so Himself: "I and the Father are one" (John 10:30 NIV).

Jesus wanted people to understand that His union with the Father was what gave Him the ability to function in the pure design of what God had intended every human being to enjoy.

> Do you not believe that I am in the Father, and the Father in Me? The words that I speak to you I do not speak on My own authority; but the Father who dwells in Me does the works. Believe Me that I am in the Father and the Father in Me, or else believe Me for the sake of the works themselves.
>
> Most assuredly, I say to you, he who believes in Me, the works that I do he will do also; and greater works than these he will do. (John 14:10–12)

Man was originally created to enjoy fellowship and intimacy with the Father, but that proximity was interrupted by Adam and Eve's sin. Jesus came to show us that this could once again be possible and we could have and enjoy intimacy with the Father.

Through Christ, we have *proximity* and *immediacy*. Our connection with God is perfect. "Religion," that imitation of true Christianity, thrives on *distance* and *delay*.

In the New Testament, there is an ever-present awareness of the awesome truth that God has made His abode in us. It's an awareness of union with Him. The Spirit of God is depicted as being present and ready to hear our call. Anyone who talks about God being distant or deaf does not share in the same Spirit we find in the New Testament writings. Those writings overflow with a rich awareness that God has restored the union with us He always desired.

When Jesus spoke to His disciples just before He laid down His life, the focus of His communication to the disciples turned to the theme of the privilege that was about to become theirs: reunion to relationship with the Father.

> Let not your heart be troubled; you believe in God, believe also in Me. In My Father's house are many mansions; if it were not so, I would have told you. I go to prepare a place for you. And if I go and prepare a place for you, I will come again and receive you to Myself; that where I am, there you may be also. And where I go you know, and the way you know. (John 14:1–4)

Jesus wasn't talking about a construction site in heaven. He has the ability to create with one word, so He's not overseeing some building project that has occupied Him for the last two thousand years as He labored to create some nice neighborhood for us to live in. The context of this whole chapter is Jesus sharing how He is going to create access for us to the Father, as He was enjoying it here on Earth.

However, the disciples did not understand where Jesus was going or how to get there, so they asked Him about it. In His reply, He makes it clear that we *can* understand where He is going and we can know the way:

> Thomas said to Him, "Lord, we do not know *where You are going*, and how *can we know the way?*"
> Jesus said to him, "*I am the way*, the truth, and the life. No one *comes to the Father* except through Me." (John 14:5–6)

We can know where Jesus is going because He declares His destination: *the Father*. And we can know the path to that destination because Jesus declares the way: *through Jesus Himself.*

> But now in Christ Jesus you who once were far off *have been brought near* by the blood of Christ. (Eph. 2:13)

It is in this intimate relationship with God that our lives fundamentally change and we start living in a new way. We saw earlier that there was something unique in how Jesus spoke, prayed, handled challenges, and engaged people. When we enter into this new life with Him, the way *we* speak, pray, handle challenges, and engage people will change as well. These things will be fundamentally altered when you live with the awareness of God's fullness in your life. You now do life differently. This is the basis of how we will deeply affect our world.

This is what Jesus said to Philip when he challenged Jesus, still wanting to somehow reach out to see the Father and not recognizing that the Father was already present in what Jesus was doing:

> "If you had known Me, you would have known My Father also; and from now on you know Him and have seen Him."
>
> Philip said to Him, "Lord, show us the Father, and it is sufficient for us."
>
> Jesus said to him, "Have I been with you so long, and yet you have not known Me, Philip? He who has seen Me has seen the Father; so how can you say, 'Show us the Father'?" (John 14:7–9)

Jesus reinforced *this* message, this understanding of His own intimate relationship with the Father, to the disciples as the most important thing He could communicate just before laying down His life. He wanted them to remember His intimacy with the Father, because He was about to establish that same intimacy as the privilege of all mankind.

Count how many times Jesus emphasized that intimacy with the word *in*.

> Do you not believe that I am *in* the Father, and the Father *in* Me? The words that I speak to you I do not speak on My own authority; but the Father who dwells *in* Me does the works. Believe Me that I am *in* the Father and the Father *in* Me, or else believe Me for the sake of the works themselves. (John 14:10–11)

This was a radical statement. The Jewish religious establishment of the day could not accept that a human being could place himself in any kind of relational intimacy with God. To them, God was a consuming fire, as unapproachable as a tornado. Even today, many religious people refer to the *transcendence* of God, that God is almighty and all-powerful but untouchable, but they do not know the *immanence* of God, that He becomes very present and approachable, having made His residence in us.

When Jesus came, He introduced a totally new framework for relating to God. In the New Testament, God no longer bestows His nearness on us on the basis of our good performance; He comes to make His home in us, not because we deserve it but because He has decided it.

> And I will pray the Father, and He will give you another Helper, that He may abide with you forever—the Spirit of truth, whom the world cannot

receive, because it neither sees Him nor knows Him; but you know Him, for He *dwells* with you and will be *in* you. I will not leave you orphans; *I will come to you.*

A little while longer and the world will see Me no more, but *you will see Me.* Because I live, you will live also. (John 14:16–19)

At that day you will know that I am *in* My Father, and you *in* Me, and I *in* you....

If anyone loves Me, he will keep My word; and My Father will love him, *and We will come to him and make Our home with him.* (John 14:20, 23)

God desires to be in us. We are the natural environment He designed for Himself. He chose humanity as His place to reside. His ultimate intention was never for His Word to be contained only in a book or a doctrine but for it to be expressed in human form. The physical body of Jesus did not restrict God. In fact, He found full expression in Him. Jesus on Earth was the exact expression of the invisible God revealed in a human body.

Conversely, God Himself is also the natural environment in which humanity is to live. God is in us, and we are in Him. What an unrestricted environment He gave us. He is our comfort zone.

For in Him we live and move and have our being. (Acts 17:28)

We are to become comfortable in Him, just as He is comfortable and at home in us. We are His holy temple, and He is the grace environment in which we live. He is our natural habitat, the environment we were created for, and vice versa.

You are designed for intimacy with the Father. You are His chosen "structure." You are His mobile temple, and He desires no other dwelling.

You are the Father's chosen address on Earth.

As city changers, we engage our world, our communities, and our cities differently when we understand the glorious unity we now have with God.

Integrity

On the basis of our understanding of our true *identity* in Christ and our privilege of sharing *intimacy* with God, we now live in a new way, which we can refer to as *integrity*.

Humanity is so overwhelmed by the consequences of the fall of Adam that they do not recognize the implications of the triumph of Christ. Jesus's victory through the cross and resurrection is one in which humanity has been included, and it far exceeds the implications of Adam's fall. Through faith, we can now live the way Jesus lived when He walked in the flesh here on Earth. The difference between Jesus Christ and us, in terms of living a victorious life of integrity, is His understanding of who He was and His awareness of the presence of the Father.

Identity precedes activity—the way you see yourself determines how you live!

Walking Worthily

Paul writes this in Ephesians:

> I, therefore, the prisoner of the Lord, beseech you
> to walk worthy of the calling with which you were
> called. (Eph. 4:1)

Let's unpack this verse a little, because it holds a key for us. The Greek word behind the English word *worthy* is *axios. Axios* means

- "weighing, having weight, *having the weight of another thing of like value*, worth as much
- befitting, congruous, corresponding to a thing."[3]

I emphasized the phrase that is most pertinent to us here. If I put that definition into Paul's sentence in place of the word *worthy*, we find that we are to walk as if we have the same weight of the calling with which we are called.

In the Old Testament, the Hebrew word often used for *righteousness* is *tsedeq*, which refers to the crossbeam on a scale of balances. If Christ is the standard of measurement and He is placed on one side of a scale, then the only thing that will balance the scale will be something that reflects His likeness and image. That's who we are in our inner, redeemed selves, and keeping that image in mind will help us live more godly lives as we walk the streets of Babylon.

Christ is the measure of our integrity. This is why Paul spent the first three chapters of his letter to the Ephesian church communicating to them their true identity and position in Christ.

Temptation tampers with our integrity. But temptation is temptation only when your spiritual identity is leaning toward accepting an inferior identity. Temptation would convince you of shortcoming, lack, need, and imperfection. But the wisdom that comes from above persuades you of your fullness and completeness in Christ.

Embracing the truth of your "spirit identity" as revealed in Christ is what empowers you to overcome temptation. It becomes your armor and weaponry to stand when attacks come your way.

> Finally, my brethren, be strong in the Lord and in the power of His might. Put on the whole armor of God, that you may be able to stand against the wiles of the devil. For we do not wrestle against flesh and blood, but against principalities, against powers, against the rulers of the darkness of this age, against spiritual hosts of wickedness in the heavenly places. Therefore take up the whole armor of God, that you may be able to withstand in the evil day, and having done all, to stand. (Eph. 6:10–13)

As we deal with temptation by putting on the armor of God (recognizing who we are in Christ), we acknowledge that we have been empowered—not just to qualify for heaven but also to be part of God's mission here on Earth. Therefore, we embrace the good news of the gospel to live in a new way as we engage everyday life.

But we need to wake up to the glorious reality that we partake in the unsearchable riches of Christ. This will deeply affect our lives and change the way we live. With this conviction, we are ready to engage a hostile and broken world.

When we know who we are in Christ and when we live with the constant awareness of God's presence, we're city changers, bringing His presence into our world, and we're ready to be a redemptive presence in Babylon.

3

A NEW BANDWIDTH
IN MY THEOLOGY

Action flows from what we believe. If we want to change our activity, we must change our convictions.

When the Doxa Deo leadership team and I began thinking about how to engage our city, we quickly realized there were two primary areas in which we would have to change: our theology and our philosophy. In the next two chapters, we'll explore those changes.

The first area we had to change was our theology.

Moving Theologically

Unfortunately, despite having gone through extensive theological training, I had ended up with a very narrow view of God's full redemption story. I had a conviction of the need to introduce people to personal redemption, but I knew very little of how Christ had reconciled *all* things to God.

For it pleased the Father that in Him all the fullness
should dwell, and *by Him to reconcile all things to
Himself,* by Him, whether things on earth or things
in heaven. (Col. 1:19–20)

I now have a more complete understanding of redemption,
which includes a desire not only to spend eternity with God but also
to embrace truth that will empower me to represent the kingdom of
God here in the world right now. Your personal discovery of your
true identity and restoration to intimacy with God now embraces
God's agenda for a broken and damaged world. It is critical to have
a holistic view of redemption, which includes personal salvation and
also the redemption of the cosmos.

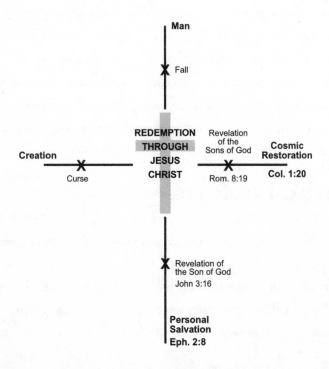

When Jesus paid the price for redemption, He paid the full price for both personal salvation and cosmic restoration. The key to our personal salvation, we know, is in the revelation of God's love through His Son. The key to the restoration of creation is in us as the redeemed children of God, now colaboring with Christ to effect the transformation.

> The earnest expectation of the creation eagerly waits
> for the revealing of the sons of God. (Rom. 8:19)

I was convinced the church needed a very strong evangelistic engagement with people. I was committed to ensuring their personal redemption. If I was going to change the world, I thought, it would be through introducing people to this new life in Christ. My theory was that if people could be transformed and have a life-giving relationship with Jesus Christ, they would leave some positive residue in the world. And of course, in this there is some truth.

Although I am convinced that only a transformed life will deeply affect the world with kingdom life, not all Christ followers share this sense of mission. Not all of them understand their calling as "sons" of God. (The concept of "sonship" in Scripture implies the coming of age—having gone through the adoption of the sonship ceremony, to be established as an heir of the estate. There is a distinct difference in the concepts "child" and "son"—see Gal. 4:1–7.) An increase in the number of Christians in a culture does not necessarily result in a transformed environment. I suspect this comes from being conditioned to believe that we have no role to fulfill in the world as it relates to transformation and that our only purpose is to wait for Christ to return, when we can escape to another reality. I began to wonder to what extent this theological premise was the reason we did not typically have all Christ followers living with the glorious understanding that we are called to be instruments of transformation within our world.

I was aware that in some of the more classical expressions of Christianity, transformation seemed to focus on a social justice agenda. My own bent had been to concentrate on people's personal redemption and their restored relationship with God rather than any form of social engagement. This, of course, led the evangelical community sometimes to posturing and speaking out against other well-meaning Christian endeavors if they were focusing on "daily bread" rather than the "Bread of Life" or on the homeless rather than on us finding our home in God.

Growing up and in my early years of ministry, it always seemed as if the Christian fraternity were fragmented as each group protected its own portion of the gospel story. Sometimes they even seemed to be in contradiction to one another. You could say I didn't exactly grow up with a theology that encouraged me to be out engaging the world. I actually grew up not liking the world. I was trained not to associate myself with the world but rather was encouraged to keep a good distance from it. I was convinced that the basic premise of the gospel was to get people out of the world.

One of my favorite scriptures was "I am not of the world" (John 17:16).

To me, it meant that Jesus Himself didn't really like the world and wanted us to distance ourselves from it. That was how I went through my young life … until one day when I read this verse in context.

In John 17, I discovered, Jesus was praying just before He was crucified. He said He was not praying for the disciples only but also for all who are far off who would one day believe in His Word. In essence, Jesus was including us in this prayer.

> *I do not pray that You should take them out of the world,* but that You should keep them from the evil one. They are not of the world, just as I am not of the world. Sanctify them by Your truth. Your word is truth. *As You sent Me into the world, I also have sent them into the world.* (John 17:15–18)

I was stumped by what I read. How could Jesus hate the world yet not pray for His disciples to be taken out of it? If the world was bad, why *wouldn't* He pray for them to somehow be removed from it—or at least spared from it?

Instead, He prayed that they would stay in the world.

Most confusing of all was that He said He was sending them into the world in the same way He Himself had been sent into it. Almost as if they were going out into the sea to go fishing. Almost as if they had some mission. Almost as if there was something good in the world worth working for. I couldn't figure this out. It conflicted with my entire view of the world. I prayed for understanding. And one day it came … through a very unlikely source.

The Parable of the Fleas

My dog had fleas. My plan was to comb through its hair and catch every flea I could find.

I don't know whether you have tried this, but it is a very difficult exercise. As I was trying to find and catch the fleas, a friend arrived and asked what I was doing. I explained to him my project, and he looked at me strangely.

"Alan," he said, "why don't you just go buy a flea collar at the store?"

I sat stunned. What was this "flea collar" of which he spoke? What a brilliant idea!

I rushed off, bought a flea collar, and put it around the dog's neck. Within three days, the fleas were gone.

I was amazed, so I tried to figure out how the system worked. How did the fleas know there was a flea collar around the dog's neck? How did they know it was a *flea* collar? I hadn't explained it to them: "Listen here, fleas; there's a collar on the dog now, so you're going to have to leave." Yet somehow all the fleas—including the last flea at the tail end—knew there was a flea collar, and they all got off. I asked my friend to explain how the fleas knew it was time to leave.

My friend said it was actually very simple. There was powder on the flea collar. When the dog moved, its hair brushed against the collar and released the powder. The powder got onto the dog's skin and was absorbed into its bloodstream. The dog developed immunity to what was poison to the fleas. Its blood carried the flea poison to every inch of its skin. So when the flea at the tail end bit the dog, the flea died.

To my friend's surprise, I didn't say, "Thank you for explaining flea collars." Instead, I cried out, "Hallelujah! I now understand John 17!"

Because that is exactly what Jesus was praying. Here's my new translation of that verse: "Father, I do not pray that You take them out of the flea nest of this world. Instead, put them right in among the fleas."

Jesus wasn't praying for them to be excused from the world but for God to do something to them. "Sanctify them by Your truth. Your word is truth" (v. 17). He wanted truth to find opportunity in their lives because He knew truth would build an immune system within them. When truth became part of their lives, they would move through the world unaffected by its poison. Instead, they would affect their world.

Imagine the power of this truth that it can so empower you to engage a broken, damaged, and confused world and not be intimidated by or infatuated with it. The core purpose of truth is therefore not just to get people prepared for heaven but rather to empower people to live effectively in the world here and now.

Empowered by Truth

> Sanctify them by Your truth. Your word is truth.
> (John 17:17)

Jesus prayed that truth would build in the disciples' lives (and our lives) an immune system so that when they reentered the world, they would not be affected by it but would affect it instead. That is why we continue to communicate truth: so people can understand their identity in Christ, find intimacy with God, and discover their true calling in life. As they discover their purpose, they are empowered to engage and influence this world.

Many Christians believe, as I mentioned in the previous chapter, that the whole point of Christianity is to get to heaven. The great reward of coming to Christ, they think, is a mansion in the halls of eternity. But the primary reward of Christianity is the privilege of having Jesus Christ residing within us. The point of the redemption story isn't heaven as a place but the Christian's newfound seamless proximity to our heavenly Father.

It is within this new glorious union that we experience the empowerment to function in Babylon. That was the reason Jesus prayed we would be sanctified and empowered by truth. Truth is the immunization against the contamination we will contend with.

AIDS, which stands for *acquired immune deficiency syndrome,* is a physical challenge that involves a malfunctioning immune system, as the name implies. I don't mean to make light of anyone living with AIDS, but I would say that many people are suffering from a spiritual form of AIDS. Their spiritual immunities are deeply deficient.

Many people want to engage the world but do not have a clear understanding of truth. Without truth as our immunity, we cannot be salt and light to change the world—we will become like it.

When we discover the truth of who we are in Christ, we can engage Babylon and make an impact. Then we are not just good people trying to do good stuff—then we are agents of the kingdom of God engaging a world that belongs to Him.

The earth is the LORD's, and all its fullness. (Ps. 24:1)

Jesus gave us a terrific illustration of what it looks like to desire to engage our culture for God. He takes a moment to stop and look out over the city of Jerusalem. He is moved by compassion because they are rejecting Him and thus sealing their own doom. He is heartbroken for His people because they do not understand God's intention for them and their city (see Matt. 23:37–39).

This heartbreak plays itself out many times throughout biblical history. It seems that cities are often at the center of God's heart.

Sometimes in the Bible, God looks at cities and even whole nations as collectives, as single units. In the West, we tend to think of Christianity as an individualistic relationship between one person and one Savior. While that's certainly true, it's not the only way God thinks of humanity.

Could it be that Jesus meant the church to think not only in terms of personal salvation experiences and personal discipleship but also in terms of salvation and discipleship coming to whole cities? To whole nations?

Our mentality has to change. We have to stop preaching to people only to encourage them to a better life and the hope that we will all go to heaven one day. We need to empower people to affect communities, to affect their world. If we wish to navigate Babylon, our theology must move from a focus only on personal salvation to an understanding of the kingdom engaging all creation.

When we speak of the kingdom of God, we are referring to His presence, His rule, His authority, and His reign. To receive the kingdom of God is to accept God's rule here and now. When the kingdom becomes a present reality and not a future hope only, people are able to enjoy the blessings of God's rule. God has made Jesus the king of all creation, both the visible and the invisible.

All authority has been given to Me *in heaven and on
earth*. Go therefore … (Matt. 28:18–19)

The great "Hallelujah Chorus" reminds us:

> *The kingdom of this world*
> *Is become the kingdom of our Lord*
> *And of His Christ, and of His Christ*
> *And He shall reign for ever and ever*[4]

God wants us to understand how to represent His dominion over
the earth and *all* it contains. For too long, we have failed to live up
to our calling in Christ to be salt and light. Consequently, a messed-
up, immoral, out-of-focus world has produced children after its kind.
This is what we see today. There is a mandate on the church, as God's
kingdom agents, to engage communities in such a way that we will see
the glory of God manifested in every dimension and sphere of society.

Does the Church Naturally Affect Its Community?

Recently we became aware of a British journalist who studied the
impact of Christianity in cities. This journalist tried to figure out
what the effect of the church was on society in the most Christianized
city in the world. He looked for the city with the highest number
of people in church on the average Sunday, and by that (somewhat
suspect) measurement, he chose to look at the city of Dallas, Texas.

He evaluated Dallas according to quality of life, justice, equal opportunity, and many other things we might expect to see in a community influenced by Christ. The findings were so disappointing and surprising that the journalist sought out some of the key Christian pastors of the city to get their thoughts. Each of them was asked, "As a Christian leader, what is your response to the condition of your community?"

One by one, without exception, their response was some form of this: "I am a *spiritual* leader, responsible for the spirituality of my people." In other words, "The social dimension of the world is not my responsibility."[5]

The Influence of Dualistic Thinking

This story reflects the dualistic mentality in the church today. For the most part, we have unconsciously separated our spiritual lives from our everyday lives. As a philosophy, dualism says that spiritual things are inherently good and physical things are inherently bad. If we believe this, then certainly we would want to be less socially and culturally concerned and more spiritually focused, and our teaching and living would reflect the desire to escape the physical in order to become more spiritual.

That's why we can gather as the people of God to engage in worship on Sunday but leave those things behind on Monday through Saturday as we tend to the necessary evil of physical concerns in our everyday lives. There is some interaction between the physical and the spiritual, as when we solicit God's help in our trials and challenges, but our spiritual experiences don't really have a bearing on our engagement with the world we live in.

Jesus had a Jewish mind-set, so to speak, having grown up in that culture, and it was very different from the Western mind-set so many of us grew up with. The Jewish mind was holistic and integrated. The dualistic worldview, on the other hand, has its origin in Greek philosophy, which we have largely inherited in the West. This implicit division between the spiritual and the natural has caused us to embrace a theology that does not mobilize our people to engage their world. Why should we, if our focus is primarily spiritual and the prize of the gospel is salvation that takes you to heaven?

But Christ is Lord of all reality—spiritual *and physical.* He is Lord of government, Lord of business, Lord of education, and Lord of the arts, media, and society at large. Until all creation acknowledges His lordship, we will function in a society in need of His shalom. All the (very physical) spheres of society will make sense and work as they should only when they align themselves under the influence of His lordship.

We must undertake a theological journey to move from focusing only on salvation to focusing on the kingdom. Jesus is Lord of the earth as well as heaven, and it has always been His prayer that God's will is done in both places equally.

4

A CHANGED PHILOSOPHY

As city changers, instead of just hunkering down to endure, we need to change the way we approach life and ministry. We need a complete shift in how we think about church, how it functions, and what its mission is.

Fundamentally, the church does not exist for the church itself but rather to affect the world. We don't want to simply attract a crowd—we must move people in their spiritual journeys to become lovers of God and agents of change in communities. Unfortunately, most Christians are not discipled with the understanding that Christ is Lord of all. Most have only a limited knowledge of the Scriptures, consisting primarily of pet Bible verses they recite for physical, emotional, and social well-being.

This fragmented knowledge of Scripture, not understanding their new identity in Christ or Christ's rule over all things, has resulted in many believers acquiescing to secular humanistic positions in matters dealing with everyday life. They simply don't know that the Bible teaches otherwise. The voice of Christ followers has become very silent within the various spheres of society. How they live their lives and conduct their everyday business has little to do with their relationship with Jesus Christ and much to do with secular society and its norms and values. This raises the question of whether the church is being effective in its discipling of people.

The church is the instrument through which God wants to influence the world. But today the church finds itself relegated to dealing only with so-called spiritual matters. That's why so many Christians live in ways that reflect secular society. For us to see our communities change, we first have to change. God wants to make the world a place of shalom—of forgiveness, justice, peace, well-being, blessing, and grace. And the way that He wants to do that is through us as His representatives here on Earth. Every Christ follower is called to play a role in this mission.

Who Raises the Village?

Perhaps you have heard the African saying "It takes a village to raise a child." Your environment, the context in which you live, has a powerful influence on your worldview, your beliefs, your values, and even your behavior. You are a product of the culture you grew up in. How you do things is deeply influenced by your "village," the context in which you find yourself.

If it is true that it takes a village to raise a child, then who raises the village?

Who or what shapes the force that shapes you and me? Who has the primary influence on our villages? Who gives the village its values and its primary cultural expression? Who determines the governing influences of our society?

If the church is absent in this dialogue, then secular humanistic values will be the primary influence defining our world.

At Doxa Deo, we firmly believe the church, called as an agent of the kingdom of God, is responsible. The environment our children grow up in leaves its marks on their lives. Therefore, the condition of the village plays a fundamental part in their spiritual and social development.

We have to live within the context of the world that is shaped by the people we share everyday life with. Unfortunately, over the last few generations, for the most part we have watched the gradual deterioration of our precious villages. I believe there is hardly a village in which we live that is not in deep need of renovation: physically, socially, economically, and spiritually.

How can the village be rescued? Who or what will it take to raise the village? There can be only one answer: it takes the church to raise a village!

If the church is to raise the village, it must stop just *having* church and start *being* the church. The church must come out from behind its walls and begin to influence the village by actively engaging every component of society, ringing blessing through a display of the love of Christ and a demonstration of His power.

We need a fresh commitment to raising the standard of life in the village rather than maintaining our religious status quo. The church must rise up and shake off our indifference and face the challenges before us. We have a mandate to touch the world, and that begins with our own villages.

Our dream is to make cities places where God's presence is evident in all spheres of society so that we see the tangible effect of the reign of Christ!

Now, if you think as I did some years ago, the notion that the church can bring transformation to a region might almost make you laugh. The church? The church might influence its members and might participate in benevolent ministries across the city, but it's not as though it's a major shaper of the culture. Right?

We must discover that not only does the church have the opportunity and privilege of getting involved in forming the value system of our villages but we also have the mandate and obligation as Christ followers to define how education, media, the arts, business, government, and all the spheres of society should function.

For many years, the church has disengaged from the world and has therefore become marginalized. In many places around the world, the church has become a peripheral activity. It is a little subculture doing its own thing, disengaged from the culture of the day.

That was never God's plan for the church.

> All this energy issues from Christ: God raised him
> from death and set him on a throne in deep heaven,
> in charge of running the universe, everything from
> galaxies to governments, no name and no power
> exempt from his rule. And not just for the time
> being, but *forever*. He is in charge of it all, has the
> final word on everything. At the center of all this,

Christ rules the church. *The church, you see, is not peripheral to the world; the world is peripheral to the church.* The church is Christ's body, in which he speaks and acts, by which he fills everything with his presence. (Eph. 1:20–23 THE MESSAGE)

Our world—this Babylon we call home—can be understood only in relation to God through Jesus Christ. The church fails if it presents Christianity as an alternative activity that has no relation to our everyday life. Christianity must be depicted as a life system that governs every area of society's functioning. We need to see (and show) Christ in every aspect of life. If we miss detecting His influence in any of the spheres of society, we lose the harmony of a well-functioning community. We lose the shalom, or wholeness quotient, of the city. The church is called as a missional presence to inculcate the character of Christ into the core of the community.

Christianity is a comprehensive, life-giving framework of truth that, when embraced, will have a redemptive effect on the culture. From the beginning of the Bible to the end, it is clear that our loving God includes all creation in His kingdom. Christ's victory did not pertain to a few Christians only but to every community and city and nation that will ever be. We must see Christ as the all-encompassing truth, the defining reference of all functions of society.

From Inward to Outward

We as the leaders at Doxa Deo began employing this thinking. We had to first believe that Christ has redeemed all things. We knew we could either honor Him in all things or soon lose sight of His presence in anything.

> For it pleased the Father that in Him all the fullness should dwell, and by Him to *reconcile all things* to Himself, by Him, whether *things on earth* or things in heaven. (Col. 1:19–20)

We had to shift from the idea that we are simply pastoring a church to the thought that we are actually pastoring a community. When that notion first hit us, it felt overwhelming. Remember the Jews who had been conquered and exiled to Babylon? Remember how their captors asked them to sing some of the songs of Zion (see Ps. 137:3)? Remember how those Jews felt when Jeremiah told them they weren't going home anytime soon and should turn their best energies to seeking the good of the hostile, godless nation they found themselves in (see Jer. 29:5–7)? Yes, that's pretty much how we felt when we realized God was asking us to become pastors of our city.

Yet God's call is for us to go beyond church growth and settle for nothing short of our communities reflecting in various ways the presence of Christ. The church needs a clear vision not only for bringing people into the fold but also for releasing them into the world. This requires a move from a pastoral/inward paradigm to a missional/ outward paradigm.

Now, unquestionably, the church must pastor the people of God. What I'm saying is that the pastoring role should find its expression in a greater mission of desiring to change the context in which the people we pastor live. No longer are we only trying to save those who are drowning; we are also to go upstream to keep people from being pushed into the stream in the first place.

Our cities are at great risk, and the church must step up to meet the challenge. If we are to align ourselves with the mission of God, we must begin to close the gap between the current reality and God's vision for our cities.

Because of the urgency of the moment and the opportunity before us, the church must begin to do its work in a fresh and new way. We have to change our philosophy of ministry. We have to start thinking differently about church, and we have to start thinking differently about the people *in* the church. We must realize that God wants to do something in Babylon through His people. Both the church leadership and the church members themselves must come to church not only to be *blessed* but primarily to be *equipped*.

Church can be the place where basic training is given to new recruits. It can be the forward operating base in a theater of battle. It can be officers' training school and the war college. It can be a field hospital and a rally point and an armory and a motor pool. But in all those word pictures, the common idea is that the church serves people whose main job it is to leave there and get back into the fight.

God wants to significantly influence culture through people's lives. This is the notion behind the raising of city changers. So now, if a woman is a teacher, she is going back into Babylon on Monday, and we need to commission her to carry the shalom (the completeness, wholeness, and harmony) of God with her into the school environment. All the members in your church need to understand that they, too, are called and that the church is there to equip and commission them to go and affect every sphere of society, whether the classroom or the boardroom, with the mandate of seeing the kingdom of God come into their particular area of influence. They are therefore no longer just passive attending members; they now become partners of the dream to see a community or city transformed. They are called ones!

The Eight Spheres

If we're going to influence every aspect of our communities, we need a working knowledge of what those aspects are. The Doxa Deo leadership team considered the functioning of our city, Pretoria, South Africa, which is the nation's capital and has approximately 2.5 million people living in its greater metro area. And in 1996, we identified eight primary spheres of activity in our "village":

1. Church
2. Business
3. Education
4. Sports
5. Social Services
6. Media
7. Arts and Culture
8. Government

These eight spheres, when functioning well, form the basis of a healthy community. They can be categorized into four primary areas of focus:

1. Healthy Spirituality
2. Healthy Mentality
3. Healthy Productivity
4. Healthy Lifestyle

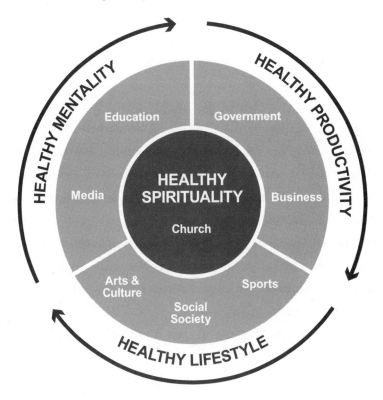

We are aware that other ministries have identified other expressions of these spheres or domains of society, and we have great appreciation for their efforts as well. But these eight areas of focus have served us well for the last twenty-plus years.

If we were going to become city changers, we knew we needed to influence all eight of those centers of a community's activity. We asked ourselves, "How can we engage in each of these spheres, trusting that Christ's presence will find opportunity and manifestation in every one of these dimensions of our community?"

Toward the end of His life, Jesus prayed this to His Father:

> I have brought you glory on earth by finishing the
> work you gave me to do. (John 17:4 NIV)

Jesus knew what His job was, and He did it. His Father had sent Him to accomplish specific objectives. He knew what they were, and He completed them. Like Jesus, our job on Earth is to flourish within the space of our personal, family, vocational, and civic environments. We must live in such a way that our spirituality is expressed in all our everyday activities.

The Old Testament book of Leviticus records an amazing promise of blessing and grace that God offers His people. This sevenfold promise encompasses every aspect of societal engagement.

> I will send the rains in their seasons, the ground
> will yield its crops and the trees of the field their
> fruit. You will thresh until the grape harvest and
> the grape harvest will continue until planting time;
> you'll have more than enough to eat and will live
> safe and secure in your land.
>
> I'll make the country a place of peace—you'll
> be able to go to sleep at night without fear; I'll
> get rid of the wild beasts; I'll eliminate war. You'll
> chase out your enemies and defeat them: Five of

you will chase a hundred, and a hundred of you will chase ten thousand and do away with them. I'll give you my full attention: I'll make sure you prosper, make sure you grow in numbers, and keep my covenant with you in good working order. You'll still be eating from last year's harvest when you have to clean out the barns to make room for the new crops.

I'll set up my residence in your neighborhood; I won't avoid or shun you; I'll stroll through your streets. I'll be your God; you'll be my people. (Lev. 26:4–12 THE MESSAGE)

In this promise to His people, God presents seven categories of blessing and health that He longs to bestow on His people. We can accept that God wants to bless every environment in this way, even Babylon.

- God wants to bless our regions with *ecological health*: "I will send the rains in their seasons, the ground will yield its crops and the trees of the field their fruit" (v. 4 THE MESSAGE).
- God wants to bless our regions with *economic health*: "You will thresh until the grape harvest and the grape harvest will continue until planting time; you'll have more than enough to eat and will live safe and secure in your land" (v. 5 THE MESSAGE).

- God wants to bless our regions with *personal security*: "I'll make the country a place of peace—you'll be able to go to sleep at night without fear" (v. 6a THE MESSAGE).
- God wants to bless our regions with *civil security*: "I'll get rid of the wild beasts; I'll eliminate war" (v. 6b THE MESSAGE).
- God wants to bless our regions with *regional security*: "You'll chase out your enemies and defeat them: Five of you will chase a hundred, and a hundred of you will chase ten thousand and do away with them" (vv. 7–8 THE MESSAGE).
- God wants to bless our regions with *prosperity*: "I'll give you my full attention: I'll make sure you prosper, make sure you grow in numbers, and keep my covenant with you in good working order. You'll still be eating from last year's harvest when you have to clean out the barns to make room for the new crops" (vv. 9–10 THE MESSAGE).
- God wants to bless our regions with *His presence*: "I'll set up my residence in your neighborhood; I won't avoid or shun you; I'll stroll through your streets. I'll be your God; you'll be my people" (vv. 11–12 THE MESSAGE).

These are not just spiritual blessings. These are the blessings to your own community.

God's engagement with us does not end with our spiritual life. It encompasses every area of our functioning. Therefore, God wants us to become equipped not only to survive but also to thrive within our world. We must change our philosophy about how we as God's people engage our world.

5

A NEW UNDERSTANDING OF THE WORLD

I grew up thinking I was supposed to brace myself against the hostility of the wicked world, so it was quite a shock to realize I was supposed to start feeling love and compassion for it.

For many, the pressure to engage a dark and dangerous world results in either an extreme position against it or an abandonment of their previous convictions. We don't want Christians abandoning their faith for any reason! Christianity, truly understood, is completely harmonious with love for the world. Not the system of the world, which is the very thing that we want to change, but the world that God loved so much He sent His Son to redeem it.

We need to discover God's deep love for the world. When John wrote that "God so loved the world" (John 3:16), he was referring to God's love for humanity. This is the same humanity that deserved judgment and death. But now, thanks to what God did in Christ, humanity deserves nothing less than to hear the glorious good news of the redemption that has been made available to them.

> Now all things are of God, who has reconciled us to Himself through Jesus Christ, and has given us the ministry of reconciliation, that is, that God was in Christ reconciling the world to Himself, not imputing their trespasses to them, and has committed to us the word of reconciliation. (2 Cor. 5:18–19)

In the very early days of the church, the apostle Peter discovered—somewhat to his horror—that what happened when the Lamb of God was slain was of far greater consequence than his old system of theology had allowed him to see:

> And a voice spoke to him again the second time, "What God has cleansed you must not call common." (Acts 10:15)

What a blow that must have been to a good Jew like Peter, who had lived his life abiding by the Old Testament rules about what God considered clean and unclean. Those rules pertained to food, to animals, and to humans. And now God was asking him to throw all that out? He was to discover that what God has cleansed we may no longer call unclean.

God calls things clean, even things that might seem unclean to us, not because He is taking a chance but because He knows the truth. Christ paid the price so that redemption could be offered to all. Faith is to see what God sees in the once-and-for-all sacrifice of Jesus on behalf of all humanity.

Romans 4:25 says Christ was put to death *because of* our offenses but was raised *because of* our justification. If God did not believe that the death of His Son was sufficient to deal with our sin and restore us to righteousness, Jesus would not have been raised. But now, since He was raised from the dead, we are included in that conviction God has regarding mankind.

It was on these grounds that God told Peter he could no longer call any human unclean. What happened to calling certain things and people unclean and unholy? By Christ's death, the cancelation of those condemnations occurred. Blood was shed through the most perfect sacrifice, never to be repeated. Through it, God acquitted the human race even while they were still hostile toward Him.

> For if when we were enemies we were reconciled
> to God through the death of His Son, much more,
> having been reconciled, we shall be saved by His
> life. (Rom. 5:10)

Now we have great confidence to appeal to the consciences of all people to realize the truth that they are already redeemed and forgiven! Don't hear me wrong: every individual still must come to Christ by faith and receive Him as Savior and Lord. I don't mean to say that all people are already saved. What I do mean is that now, thanks to Christ's completed work of redemption, all mankind *may* receive salvation if they come to Him by faith.

Grace and Truth

While Jesus was here on Earth, He managed to interact in this very broken, damaged, and sinful world with ease and without compromise. He was the most holy person to ever live, yet He effortlessly connected with people who carried some of the worst societal labels. Tax collectors and prostitutes were among those He found a comfort level with.

We want to emulate the strategy of Jesus, which seemed to fully integrate the concepts of grace and truth. In every interaction Jesus had with people, it was obvious that He first embraced them in grace. While society might have condemned them for their sin or their choices or their illnesses and dispositions, Jesus received them in grace. Only later would He share truth.

He didn't skip over the truth, and that's an important point. But so many of us lead with truth and think to offer grace later, maybe. We want people to change their ways first and thus earn grace. But Christ accepted people in all their brokenness, which made their melting hearts receptive to His loving words of correction.

Grace attempts to meet people where they are. It seeks to understand before asking to be understood. Grace knows that people need love the most when they deserve it the least. Grace is an environment in which people feel acceptance and worth rather than judgment and condemnation.

We are purveyors of grace. We carry this glorious message of God's love to humanity. Therefore, we need to see ourselves as environmental engineers of grace. We need to construct environments where people feel safe to hear the truth that can set them free, and these environments are built when we first offer grace.

And the Word became flesh and dwelt among us,
and we beheld His glory, the glory as of the only
begotten of the Father, full of grace and truth....
For the law was given through Moses, but grace
and truth came through Jesus Christ. (John 1:14, 17)

First grace, then truth.

When Jesus spoke with the Samaritan woman at the well (see John 4:1–30), He said that if she knew the generosity of God and who He really was, she would ask and receive living water. He offered her a great gift but hadn't said a word about her lifestyle, though it quickly became clear He knew all about her brokenness. First He created a sense that she was invited into the grace of God, sharing a vision that God's generosity was open to her and that living water could flow from her life as well. Only after He had established that God's love was available to her did Jesus directly address the brokenness in her life.

She replied with a religious argument about the "proper" place to worship God. Jesus responded by revealing yet another dimension of God's grace, which is to worship Him in spirit and truth, regardless of the location.

The woman had been on her guard about conversing with a Jewish rabbi, since most of them would have spurned her outright, not only because she was a woman but also because she was Samaritan—and if they'd known about her past, they would've rejected her even more quickly and thoroughly. Then, when He hadn't rejected her outright, she still felt defensive and tried to move the conversation into the realm of argument.

By refusing to reject her or get derailed into debate and by extending God's grace to this woman, Jesus was able to move her from enemy to follower in a single short conversation. She left that well and went back to the village, where she shared with everyone what had transpired, resulting in people mobilized and willing to come and engage Jesus and hear the good news He offered them.

In the story of the woman caught in adultery, we see another example of how Jesus first established grace and then shared truth (see John 8:3–11). The Pharisees who brought this woman before Jesus wanted her to be condemned and executed on the spot. They had their own merciless ideas of justice. Of course, they also wanted to trap Jesus, knowing He was obligated to share their stand on this doctrine. They knew He wouldn't want to have her stoned to death, but they hoped either to force Him to do so in order to obey the traditional teachings or to force Him to disobey those teachings, which would expose Him as a lawbreaker.

Jesus knew their trick, and He stunned them with this brilliant response: "He who is without sin among you, let him be the first to throw a stone at her" (v. 7 NASB).

In reality, Jesus was the only one qualified to throw the first stone. He was the only one without sin, after all. By reminding them of their own sin and therefore the punishment that could just as easily come on them, He neatly stepped out of their trap. After they had all departed, leaving Jesus alone with the woman, He said He wouldn't condemn her. But He didn't just wink at her sin. After protecting her with grace, He spoke truth: "From now on sin no more" (v. 11 NASB).

May we do the same as we interact with the citizens of Babylon around us. Because except for the grace of God, we might be among them and still have never heard that grace is available even to us.

The Church's Relation to the World

Over the years and around the world, the church has had a variety of approaches to Babylon. On one extreme might be convents and monasteries and Amish communities, where the idea is to withdraw from the world as much as possible. On the other end of the spectrum might be those so willing to surrender and compromise that there's no visible difference between them and the world around them.

I would argue that neither extreme allows Christians to truly be salt and light to the world. How can you be salt if you're not sprinkled onto the meat at all—or are so similar to the meat that the salt has lost its saltiness? And how can you be light if you've either hidden the light away from the world or dimmed it so much that it doesn't stand out?

As I survey Christian communities and their engagement with the world, I see these primary approaches.

The Protesting Church

Christians who believe the world is an evil place and needs to be challenged in a very visible and loud way choose protest as the way to engage. Picket lines, demonstrations, and public protests are the hallmarks of this approach.

There's no denying that this approach garners attention and media exposure. Consequently, many people outside the church come to believe that Christians are all about what they hate and whom they condemn.

The Absent Church

Here the Christian community seeks to isolate itself and avoid the mainstream environment. They may not retreat to a cloistered community, but neither do they roll up their sleeves and work in the streets and alleys of Babylon.

Once the church abdicates its role in society, society quickly moves on without it. It could be argued that this is the situation we see in many places in the world. In the eyes of the culture, if the church does anything at all, it's confined to "irrelevant" matters of religion and so-called spirituality.

Not only is the church itself disengaged in this approach, but individual Christians also keep their beliefs to themselves as they walk the world's byways. Consequently, although we have millions of Christians serving in secular society and while numbers of people are attending Sunday church services, our presence has almost no impact and our culture continues to reflect a secular and humanistic worldview.

The Cultural Church

Now the pendulum swings toward the other side. Here the church does indeed engage society but to the extent that it assimilates the value system of Babylon so it's indistinguishable from the world and therefore has no influence and does not affect the way the culture functions.

Unfortunately, we have mentioned that many Christians don't have a biblical worldview but only a cursory knowledge of pet Bible verses they recite for physical and emotional health. If a church is mostly filled with such immature believers, there may be a desire not to represent your convictions publicly, especially if doing so would make someone else feel judged or would result in some form of persecution for the believer. This limited, fragmented demonstration of life in Christ has resulted in believers and churches acquiescing to secular humanistic views in all practical matters pertaining to our economic, civil, and social functioning.

The Incarnational Church

This is the approach we would like all churches around the world to take. It's the one I believe churches must adopt if we are to have any hope of transforming Babylon. In the incarnational approach, the church becomes a wholesome engager of the world—from inside it.

Usually churches try to find a mission and ask God to bless it. But the incarnational approach to transforming our communities and cities acknowledges that God already has a plan, is already present in the world, and invites the church to join Him in carrying out His plan. To participate in that mission is to participate in *the movement of God's love toward people.*

At its heart, the incarnational approach to the world is the one we saw in the life and ministry of Jesus. He didn't stand outside the culture, condemning it and waiting for it to change. Neither did

He hide His distinctiveness so no one would know He was different and had a relationship with God. He entered our world and walked among us, but He did so in a way that showed He was about God's purposes. He did this by showing grace before truth. That's the approach we need to adopt.

For the church to influence every realm of culture as salt and light, believers must learn to think in a Christ-centered way and articulate life-giving principles in the language of contemporary hearers. It's nice to have Christians in positions of influence, but we are in need of more Christian thinking in those areas of influence.

History is filled with stories of believers taking the lead in secular society and redeeming cultures for the glory of God. Two clear examples are William Penn with the Quaker movement in America and John Wesley with the Methodist movement in Britain.

Since Quakers believe that change is possible for anyone, a primary focus since their early history has been reforming criminal justice systems. They have advocated for improving prison conditions, providing education for prisoners, and many other reforms that increase the probability of positive change.

In his new colony of Pennsylvania, William Penn, the first major Quaker prison reformer, stated that "prisons shall be workhouses," that "bail should be allowed for minor offences," and that "all prisons shall be free, as to fees, food and lodgings." The only crime punishable by death was murder, and prisoners learned honest trades before being released. These reforms, radical for that era, reflected his Quaker belief in equality and cultivating "that of God" in everyone.[6]

Some believe that without the church, especially the Methodist Church, Britain might have experienced the devastating results of an uprising similar to the French Revolution. Instead, the influence of the Methodists led to extensive social reform during the Industrial Revolution, and as a result, two leaders of the movement changed history: George Whitefield and John Wesley.[7]

With so many Christians already in influential positions in society, we face not a lack of Christian presence but a lack of Christian influence. What we need is for those well-placed believers to bring their Christian thinking into these realms. We need to be, and in many cases we already are, present in every sphere of society. And we need to "lean in" with godly principles, but without clouding things with religious posturing.

In but Not Of

This is the incarnation principle: if they see us being present and different, the citizens of Babylon may wish to become what we are. But if they don't see us, they cannot be us. We need to immerse ourselves in our culture. In the world, but not of the world! How is this possible?

It all starts when you deeply understand the redemption in your own life.

This leads to the discovery that God wants to work not only in us but also through us. We discover the joy of living beyond ourselves. We become motivated by compassion, with a new desire to contribute to the needs of our culture by giving of the time, talent, and treasure that God has entrusted to us.

When we start living beyond ourselves, we discover that we are part of the greatest agenda on the planet, the *missio Dei,* the mission of God to the world. We now see Him at work in so many ways in so many different spaces and places. Jesus now seems to be everywhere. When we are fully convinced that Jesus Christ is Lord of *all,* it transforms our everyday lives. Now the spaces that occupy our days—be it the workplace, the classroom, or anywhere we go—become sacred spaces to us. They become the sections of Babylon where we are to plant gardens. We begin to seek the welfare of those spaces, knowing that they are part of the Christ-filled ecosystem we are busy establishing.

For too long, we have been under the impression that our set of dogmatic positions is the platform from which we should engage our world. If we condemn long and loud enough, the thinking goes, surely people will want to join us. I contend that what God intends for us—as His representatives on Earth—is to reveal the very life that was in Christ. To show what God is like. To lead with grace and then present truth. We serve and love and bless, and then we plead with every person to be reconciled to God.

It is an amazing thought to me that the most holy man to ever grace this planet was a friend of such very bad sinners. Could it be that people were attracted to something in Jesus that was beyond a dogmatic position? Perhaps people flocked to Him not because He got every doctrine "right" as defined by the religious elite of the day but because He gave people fountains of eternal life. That life is the very same life that God has empowered us to give the thirsty world. And when we do so, we will be as attractive to the people of Babylon as Jesus was.

Incarnation immerses itself in the real world. It is always specific to the here and now. It addresses this ordinary moment, the things right in front of us. My friend Mario is a great example of this. He shared the following:

> God can use an ordinary person to His glory in everyday circumstances, when we choose to live as those who are not of the world but are very much in the world.
>
> In 2008, when renting DVD videos was still popular, I opened a franchise for Videorama, one of the big video outlets in South Africa. As with any franchise, there are rules and regulations that owners have to abide by. As part of their framework of functioning, each store was only allowed to have a certain number of display shelves within certain categories, ensuring that every outlet would have a similar look and feel.
>
> One of the categories I was obligated to carry was an "ADULT" section that would have some very explicit titles. From the beginning, I felt very uncomfortable with this, but I had to abide by the "Franchise Agreement". So, against my will I carried these products for the first three months. I then decided to make a request of the owners of the franchise license, and I asked if I could open a "RELIGION" section. They obliged, and I then started purchasing Christian movies and populated the "RELIGION" section.

Amazingly, after three months of stocking Christian movies as an option, it became apparent that they were bringing in 60% more revenue than the "ADULT" section had brought into the store. I submitted this information to the managing director of the franchise. He was totally surprised by the results, but even bigger was my surprise, when at the next franchise meeting, he suggested that every store must create a new section for "RELIGION". This resulted in a shift so huge as the revenue of the religion section became far more profitable in all stores than the adult section, which then caused the company to discontinue the adult section. In 2017, where video shops still rent out DVDs, this company no longer carries any adult video material.[8]

Christianity speaks to real everyday life—work, finances, relationships, health, spirituality, and even entertainment. True Christianity is never irrelevant and shouldn't be considered as such. Christianity is meant to be a loving way of life, not just a system of beliefs and requirements that people hope will earn them a reward in heaven.

Jesus was concerned about the transformation of real persons and human society here on Earth; therefore, we should be too.

6

A STRATEGY FOR TRANSFORMATION

When God said He'd given me faith to trust Him for a city, I knew the Doxa Deo Church was to develop a strategy.

How does one transform a city?

One thing I knew right away: it was going to take a lot of people—including very different people—working together to pull this off.

The Feeding of the Five Thousand

Very early in the process, I felt impressed that God was telling us to look to one particular story in the Gospels for a blueprint for our strategy. Here is that story:

> Jesus, when He came out, saw a great multitude
> and was moved with compassion for them, because

they were like sheep not having a shepherd. So He began to teach them many things. When the day was now far spent, His disciples came to Him and said, "This is a deserted place, and already the hour is late. Send them away, that they may go into the surrounding country and villages and buy themselves bread; for they have nothing to eat."

But He answered and said to them, "You give them something to eat."

And they said to Him, "Shall we go and buy two hundred denarii worth of bread and give them something to eat?"

But He said to them, "How many loaves do you have? Go and see."

And when they found out they said, "Five, and two fish."

Then He commanded them to make them all sit down in groups on the green grass. So they sat down in ranks, in hundreds and in fifties. And when He had taken the five loaves and the two fish, He looked up to heaven, blessed and broke the loaves, and gave them to His disciples to set before them; and the two fish He divided among them all. So they all ate and were filled. And they took up twelve baskets full of fragments and of the fish. Now those who had eaten the loaves were about five thousand men. (Mark 6:34–44)

Notice that Jesus told the disciples to have them sit down in groups of hundreds and fifties. This is interesting to me. We can assume these people were hungry and exhausted. Many of them might've been irritated, having been in the sun all day. I wouldn't think they'd be willing to be sorted at all, much less into such defined groups.

For some reason, Jesus thought it was important to charge the disciples with the tedious exercise of getting this big mob to split into smaller groups of hundreds and fifties. They were not trained in crowd control, so can you imagine them going out to the crowd and saying, "Could you form into little groups?"

I can imagine some pushback: "What is this all about? Why do we have to do this?"

And how could the disciples answer? "Um, I *think* we're going to feed you."

"Really? How much food do you have?"

Can you imagine them trying to answer that one? Perhaps you can feel the tension of that moment. Remember, they'd wanted to send the people away. It was Jesus who wanted to keep them here and break them into groups. Perhaps He did so to create anticipation or, more strategically, to create a framework where they could monitor whether everyone had been fed.

I can just see the softhearted John: "Would you please come into groups? I am so sorry for the inconvenience. More or less fifty, if you don't mind. Yes, thank you." And then I see Peter: "Right—into groups, you lot! Fifties and hundreds. You heard me. Move, move, move! Oy, where do you think you're going?"

Unlikes Working Together

One of the amazing things in the kingdom is that God uses diversity. And one of the biggest challenges for us is to recognize the multifaceted engagement in the kingdom.

I love the diversity among the men Jesus chose as His disciples. You could not get personalities more different than Peter's and John's. And yet, when you study the Bible, you will always find Peter and John together.

And then there were Philip and Thomas, who seemed like polar opposites. Philip was a naive, easy, believe-everything disciple. Philip said, "Oh, show us the Father, and it will be enough" (see John 14:8). Jesus said, "If you have seen Me, you have seen the Father" (see v. 9). And then there was Thomas, the "show me—I want to see it myself" disciple. And guess who we find referenced together? Philip and Thomas.

The two disciples I really like are Simon the Zealot and Matthew the tax collector. They represented the two extremes of the political spectrum. On one side, you had Matthew, the sell-out tax collector. Apparently, he didn't care much for the nationalistic ideals of Israel, because his job was to take money from the people of Israel and give it to Rome. The nationalists despised and hated tax collectors.

On the other side, you had Simon the Zealot, a nationalistic patriot. The Zealots were revolutionaries with right-wing ideals, and their goal was to restore Israel's independence at any cost. If a Zealot found a tax collector alone, blood would flow.

But when Jesus chose His disciples, He decided to select one from each perspective and bring them onto the same team. I think

His sense of humor would have led to Simon and Matthew always hanging out together too!

To us, bringing such diversity together might seem impossible. But when Jesus comes into the equation, He brings different people together to share in a common mission. That's true even today. When you get on mission with God, He still brings very different people together. It's wonderful when you realize you really can work with others who might differ from you in dogmatic position but who nevertheless recognize Jesus as Lord. Even if we do not see eye to eye, we can work hand in hand.

Three Dimensions of Change

At Doxa Deo, we were compelled to get involved with other bodies of believers so we could become the Church (capital *C*) collaborating in a region. We were part of a process of bringing church leaders together to be active with us in ushering the presence of Christ into our cities, regardless of our differences.

That did not mean we sacrificed our identities or our associations with our various denominations or tribes. It meant only that we opened ourselves to new Christian relationships for impact. There are relationships for identity, and then there are relationships for impact. These were relationships in which we all pursued our common goals across three dimensions:

> **1. Spiritual.** We were aware of the "lostness" of our region, and the challenge was for us to own this as our responsibility. In most cities, if you use publicly

available data to add up those who attend church services or find the percentage of people reading the Bible and having a relationship with God and you contrast that with the number of people in the city not doing so, the results are almost always staggering. How can we change this in our region? It starts with churches coming together in unity to dialogue and embrace a shared goal to shift that percentage—then to consider remedial activities such as church planting, the nurturing of existing churches that are struggling, and outreach events.

2. Social. We must become aware of the pain of our communities. Once again, we must identify what we want to see fundamentally changed. What stubborn realities need to be addressed by a loving, Christ-centered community? This leads to the sort of compassionate involvement that creates opportunity for the church to serve the city. One of the major areas of pain around the world stems from broken families and the implications that flow socially from this. Fighting for marriage will help our communities in almost every way. According to the Institute for Family Studies, "Higher levels of marriage, and especially higher levels of married-parent families, are strongly associated with more economic growth, more economic mobility, less child poverty, and higher median family income … in the United States."[9] We need to reach out to the poor, the migrant, the homeless, and the addict. The marginalized and disenfranchised in society should be a natural focus for the church to serve.

3. Cultural. When we talk about transformation, we are talking about deeply affecting the broken components in all spheres of society. How will we cause the presence of Christ to affect all areas of culture: education, business, the arts, government, media, social services, and sports?

Outcomes vs. Activities

Understanding the difference between outputs and outcomes is important. Outputs, or *activities,* relate to what we do. *Outcomes* relate to what difference we make.

Outcomes are desired goals. They are measurable end results that matter a great deal, most times determining the well-being of the region. *Activities* are a set of tactics used to achieve those outcomes. We tend to gravitate more toward activities than outcomes. We like to be busy so we can feel that we're doing something for the greater good. But activity without a clear and desired outcome in mind might be as useless as putting up a cardboard wall to fend off a tornado.

First we need to identify the desired outcome, the goal, and then, when there is a consensus on what needs to be changed in the spiritual, social, and cultural dimensions, we can start coming up with a strategy for activities. The strategy should be one that allows collaborative engagement among all those who catch the vision to become city changers.

Planning to Succeed

Jesus told the disciples to break the groups into fifties and hundreds. We don't know why they had to break them up into groups. It could be that Jesus realized it was a good way to monitor whether everybody was getting fed. Maybe He knew it would help everyone remember how many people were there so they could accurately recount the miracle.

One thing we can say was that Jesus was preparing for a miracle so He employed His strategy. Many times in the church, we are keenly aware of the vision we want to fulfill, but we don't give enough time to establishing the strategy.

It would be very much like organizing a 5K run but not planning out the race route. There might be high interest in participating in the race, but inevitably one question is going to arise: "What route are we going to run?" Imagine if the answer from the organizer was "Just run. You know, run really fast, have a good time, and then, it's only five kilometers. It'll be great!"

We caught the vision early on: God wants to affect our city—He wants to change the community. We went out and shared that with our people, and they got all excited to do it.

But very quickly someone asked: "So what is the route? What's our strategy? How are we going to bring that vision into reality?" What if we had said, "Hey, God is giving us the city! That should be enough for you. Here are another three scriptures to confirm it"?

Too often in Christian circles, we adopt dualistic thinking that says planning and strategy are wrong. Don't think too hard about it—just go out and start doing stuff, and God will make it happen!

Indeed, in some Christian spheres, intellectual thought is almost considered the killer of the work of the Holy Spirit. Faith and analysis are seen as enemies. But God wants to give us plans, strategies, and clear directives so we can run the route. Then, within the route, we will find creative, inspirational moments when the Holy Spirit will surprise us.

We see this in the life of the Old Testament prophet Nehemiah. Nehemiah was born in Babylon during the exile. His family had been taken as captives from Jerusalem. Apparently, he lived by Jeremiah's advice and sought the good of the city, because as an adult he occupied an important position in Babylon: the king's wine taster. Few positions in the kingdom required so much trust in the people doing them. If the wine taster passed a goblet to the king, the king had to have complete faith that the taster hadn't poisoned it, because that wine went directly from the taster's hand to the king's mouth.

The exile began in 598 BC, and the protective wall around Jerusalem was torn down by Nebuchadnezzar twelve years later. After the exile stretched many years, the king allowed some Jews to go back to Jerusalem to start rebuilding it. But progress was slow and ultimately failed. Many years later, news came to Nehemiah that the conditions remained terrible in Jerusalem and the walls were still in ruins, leaving the people open to attack from enemies on all sides.

Something happened in the heart of this man. God stirred him to take responsibility to go and rebuild the wall. That was his vision—Jerusalem's wall (and its pride) restored—but he knew better than to burst through the gates and start running across the desert. He knew he first needed a strategy.

Nehemiah received this burden in the month of Chislev in the Jewish ecclesiastical calendar (November or December for us). Though the vision had to be absolutely burning in him, he dedicated the next four months to planning. Finally, in the month of Nisan (March/April), he was ready. One day the king and queen went to the summer palace to rest. That afternoon, with Nehemiah standing there serving him wine, the king smiled at the queen, and somehow Nehemiah realized it was his moment. He inhaled deeply and took the biggest risk of his life: he stood before the king with a long face.

You couldn't just do that. The king insisted everyone should look happy around him, and Nehemiah took a huge risk by looking sad. But Nehemiah had prepared, and he knew eventually he would have to take this chance if the vision were ever going to come to pass. Here he was, at the king's very elbow, with the unprecedented opportunity to try to save his people's capital.

Here is how we know that God's favor—not to mention the king's—was on Nehemiah. When he stood before the king, daring to look glum, the king noticed right away:

> Now I had never been sad in his presence before. Therefore the king said to me, "Why is your face sad, since you are not sick? This is nothing but sorrow of heart."
>
> So I became dreadfully afraid, and said to the king, "May the king live forever! Why should my face not be sad, when the city, the place of my fathers' tombs, lies waste, and its gates are burned with fire?"

> Then the king said to me, "What do you request?"
> (Neh. 2:1–4)

What would you have done in that moment, when your next words could bring about your death and the death of your vision? Nehemiah did what any sane man would've done in that situation: he prayed as if his life depended on it, and then he went for it:

> So I prayed to the God of heaven. And I said to the king, "If it pleases the king, and if your servant has found favor in your sight, I ask that you send me to Judah, to the city of my fathers' tombs, that I may rebuild it." (Neh. 2:4–5)

Imagine the pause that must've hung in the air. Not only had Nehemiah violated the king's command by appearing before him with a long face, but he also asked to go rebuild the walls of a city that the king's predecessors had destroyed—because of Jerusalem's rebellion. "Yes, O King, may I please go make your former enemy strong again? You won't mind, right?"

Finally, with the queen watching eagerly and Nehemiah probably about to pass out from fear, the king said, "How long will your journey be? And when will you return?" (Neh. 2:6).

Not "How long *would* your journey be?" but "How long *will* your journey be?" Nehemiah knew right then that the king was going to spare his life and send him to Jerusalem. With that all-or-nothing moment safely behind him, Nehemiah deployed the strategy he'd taken four months to develop. "Glad you asked, O King. Now, here's what I'll need."

> "If it pleases the king, let letters be given to me for the governors of the region beyond the River, that they must permit me to pass through till I come to Judah, and a letter to Asaph the keeper of the king's forest, that he must give me timber to make beams for the gates of the citadel which pertains to the temple, for the city wall, and for the house that I will occupy." And the king granted them to me according to the good hand of my God upon me. (Neh. 2:7–8)

Some people might hear that story and say, "Oh, wasn't that a beautiful moment the Lord created for him?" And yes, it surely was. But Nehemiah had diligently *prepared* for this moment, so when God softened the king's heart, Nehemiah was ready for the miracle.

Just as Jesus had the disciples prepare for the miracle.

The challenge for us is to prepare for the miracle. A vision needs a strategy so when God opens the door, we're ready to walk through it.

To Your Strategy, Add Commitment

Nehemiah did not know what challenges were waiting for him as he pursued his vision. He had this incredible strategy: people had to take responsibility for the portion of wall directly in front of where they lived. And in all probability, when one man saw his neighbor building the wall and realized the portion in front of his house would remain a gaping hole, he started to build his portion of the wall.

Believe it or not, some of Nehemiah's own people, including some of the Jewish nobles, did not want the wall rebuilt. But Nehemiah didn't allow this to affect him. He worked with those who wanted to work. In our day, too, opposition can derail even the grandest visions and smartest strategies. Sometimes we become so concerned about everybody who does not want to join us. The challenge is to do the work with people who have a heart to work. Even in Pretoria, we have this wonderful experience of the churches working together, but we have some churches that are not interested. So we love them, and we are pursuing the vision with those who want to work.

The challenges kept mounting against Nehemiah's life, both from within and from without. He faced opposition on every side.

"We know what your agenda is," some of his detractors said. "You want to become king. You have an ego problem." They wrote an angry letter to him (see Neh. 6:6–7), and it probably made him feel like packing up and going back to Babylon.

> They all were trying to make us afraid, saying, "Their hands will be weakened in the work, and it will not be done."
>
> Now therefore, O God, strengthen my hands.
>
> Afterward I came to the house of Shemaiah the son of Delaiah, the son of Mehetabel, who was a secret informer; and he said, "Let us meet together in the house of God, within the temple, and let us

close the doors of the temple, for they are coming to kill you; indeed, at night they will come to kill you."

And I said, "Should such a man as I flee? And who is there such as I who would go into the temple to save his life? I will not go in!" Then I perceived that God had not sent him at all, but that he pronounced this prophecy against me because Tobiah and Sanballat had hired him. For this reason he was hired, that I should be afraid and act that way and sin, so that they might have cause for an evil report, that they might reproach me. (Neh. 6:9–13)

Should a man such as Nehemiah flee when hardship comes? Of course not. Should a person such as you flee when opposition comes? Never. Add to your strategy a sense of commitment.

Nehemiah and the people rebuilt the wall in fifty-two days. It had sat in ruins, and a man with a vision, a strategy, and resolve rebuilt it in only fifty-two days. Talk about city changers!

At Doxa Deo, we've been in this journey for a quarter of a century, and we, too, are seeing the wall being built. We have committed ourselves to seeing cities transformed across the globe, because we believe God loves cities.

God's Heart for Cities

If God has a heart for people, it is obvious that He cares deeply about what happens in cities, where a major portion of the world's population lives. We have to believe that God has a strategy for His church in the city.

The church in the past did relatively well within the context of the rural setting, functioning as a strong influence within the village and town environment. The church found itself in the center of that demographic space, a reminder of its central influence on that community, governing the ebb and flow of community life and influencing the values of the community.

This changed when we moved from villages to cities. When we came to cities, the church seemed to lose its voice. It was no longer the dominant influence on values in the community. Even today Babylon seems to have overwhelmed the church. But we believe a new day is dawning for the church in the city. God is downloading a new strategy for the church to come together in unity. When we execute this strategy in alignment with the heart of God, the church will once again become the primary voice to the community. Even communities the size of Babylon.

Thank God, we are already seeing this happening. City changers are being raised. Church leaders are coming together. Leaders in business and civic society are rising to embrace a kingdom agenda. Structures of society are being changed. Babylon is being transformed.

7

PRODUCING CITY CHANGERS

When we at Doxa Deo received the word from God that He had entrusted us with the faith for a city, believing it could be transformed by His glory—indeed, that what He wanted on Earth was for all "Babylon" to be transformed by His glory—we knew we couldn't look at the members of our church (or any church) in the same way.

We realized that our people aren't coming to church to be blessed by a program.

People *are* the program.

I love this quote from Irenaeus, an early church father: *"The glory of God is man fully alive."*[10] That's what church members must be if we are to transform Babylon. As mentioned earlier, we don't refer to our church members as *members* anymore. We call them *partners*. Partners of a dream. We see them as *called ones,* having been called of God. We see them as *city changers,* as people who have an anointing on their lives to take the presence of Christ into our cities.

And now as leaders, we see ourselves empowering *them* for *their* calling. They step outside the church to engage their world as the extension of the church they belong to. They engage their everyday world as people fulfilling our church's mission in whatever they do. Now the church is in action all over the city every day, all the time.

If they happen to be teachers, for example, they now engage their classrooms, ministering to people as they relate the love and goodness of God in that space. They bring His presence into those classrooms, and that becomes the extended program of the church. Whatever transpires there, we want to celebrate when the church gathers together. We create space in our program to celebrate what God is doing through individuals in their everyday lives.

This so important: you replicate what you celebrate.

Subduing the Earth Revisited

Before the sin of Adam and Eve, God gave that first couple a command:

Fill the earth and subdue it. (Gen. 1:28)

Here's a picture of what God originally intended mankind to be doing on Earth:

Then God said, "Let Us make man in Our image, according to Our likeness; let them have dominion over the fish of the sea, over the birds of the

air, and over the cattle, over all the earth and over
every creeping thing that creeps on the earth." So
God created man in His own image; in the image
of God He created him; male and female He created them. Then God blessed them, and God said
to them, "Be fruitful and multiply; fill the earth
and subdue it; have dominion." (Gen. 1:26–28)

Not long afterward, Adam and Eve demolished that plan by
disobeying God. From the moment of the fall until the moment of
Christ's resurrection, the sin of Adam held sway over mankind and
we remained under condemnation.

But at the moment of the resurrection, redemption became
available to mankind.

When we at Doxa Deo received the vision to trust God for the
transformation of our city, we realized we needed to revisit those
verses in Genesis. Because all things had been redeemed in Christ,
we became aware that even the original mandate God had for mankind had been redeemed in Christ.

Could it be, we wondered, that He was commanding us again
to fill the earth and subdue it? Not in the political sense but in the
sense of loving, serving, and being present to create a better world.
We weren't thinking of an authoritative takeover of the world but
of a growing influence that would bring the aroma of Christ into
every area of society.

We began to recognize Jesus as Lord of all reality. And all things
in it need to recognize His lordship. Let's look at this teaching from
Paul to the Colossian church:

> [Jesus] is the image of the invisible God, the firstborn
> over all creation. For by Him all things were created
> that are in heaven and that are on earth, visible and
> invisible, whether thrones or dominions or princi-
> palities or powers. All things were created through
> Him and for Him. And He is before all things, and
> in Him all things consist. (Col. 1:15–17)

We have been crafted to display the likeness of our Maker within the uniqueness of our own ethnicity, personality, fingerprints, touch, smile, and vocal cadence. Humanity is the natural environment that God designed for Himself to live in and manifest Himself through. He chose humanity. You are His chosen location. You are the Father's address on Earth. Now we can choose to take the character and competence He empowers us with and exhibit them in a world desperate for grace and truth. We now align ourselves with God's audacious plan to deeply affect the world through ordinary people.

I find that most of humanity, especially believers, are so overwhelmed by the consequences of the fall of Adam that we have forgotten that even the fall was not great enough to compete with the impact of redemption. All humanity, and all creation, is represented in one man: Jesus!

> For if by the one man's offense death reigned
> through the one, much more those who receive
> abundance of grace and of the gift of righteousness
> will reign in life through the One, Jesus Christ.
> (Rom. 5:17)

Notice that the implications of redemption lead to a *"much more"* positioning of life than what Adam experienced. No longer is Adam the definition of our lives, but Jesus Christ Himself now defines our lives.

ROMANS 5:17

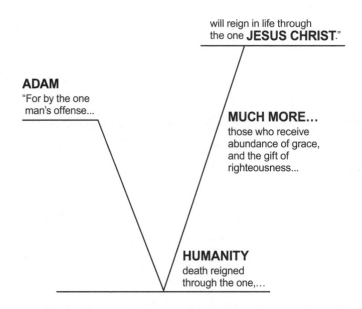

will reign in life through the one **JESUS CHRIST."**

ADAM
"For by the one man's offense...

MUCH MORE...
those who receive abundance of grace, and the gift of righteousness...

HUMANITY
death reigned through the one,...

God's ultimate intention was never for His Word to be captured only in a book or in a doctrine. Incarnation has always been His plan. His Word was always meant to become flesh so it could be expressed in human form. God wants to reveal Himself through people.

The physical body of Jesus did not restrict His divine power. In fact, God found full expression in this man. Jesus, in His person here on Earth, was the representation of the invisible God revealed in a human body. We who have embraced redemption now share this same privilege of living with the presence of God within us 24-7.

Jesus did not come to Earth to begin a religion. He came to introduce humanity to their origin. He came to reveal God's design and love for every human. He did not come to reinforce the notion that our weaknesses are the result of a faulty design but rather to announce the truth of our origin as a trophy of God's grace. He came to set us free from the false identity that we have assumed and to introduce us to our new self in Christ—to give us a new identity.

Christ came to set us free from our inferior pattern for life. He came to vindicate our design. As the final Adam of the human race, He became the proxy for every human being as the sacrificial lamb killed to rid us of our false, inferior identity in Adam. He now represents the original blueprint for our design. He represents, in Irenaeus's words, "man fully alive."

> And you shall know the truth, and the truth shall make you free.... Therefore if the Son makes you free, you shall be free indeed. (John 8:32, 36)

I think the most amazing thing about Jesus when He walked the earth was that the "worst" sinners in society were attracted to Him. Prostitutes and publicans witnessed in His life an integrity they wanted for their own. He stood holy and untouched by the world, and while He was therefore truly qualified to condemn them, He did not. He exemplified what they desired, and somehow they knew it could be true of themselves. He wanted them to realize, recognize, and appreciate that the qualities they were attracted to in Him were the very things He wanted to reproduce in them.

When God looks at us, He sees us clothed in Christ's righteous-ness. We could almost go so far as to say that God has fused us with Himself in His thought. We are not God—of course not. But to those who say God is far from us, I say the opposite. As Christ is always in and with the Father, so are we invited to be.

God established the value of humanity on the cross. If we are to create city changers in our churches, that discipling process begins by seeing God's people the way He sees them.

A New Way of Doing Discipleship

We have identified three vital principles for discipling city changers:

1. Transformational vs. Informational—Churches are agents of transformation, not just providers of information and blessing. We must be about equipping and empowering people to understand how they can manifest the Christ-life in their everyday lives. This implies that we facilitate experiential learning rather than just cognitive sharing.

2. Incarnational vs. Dualistic—City changers must come to see our communities as an integrated society where Jesus is Lord of all. We can't separate the spiritual from the natural or the "holy" from the secular. Every aspect of our lives and cities is to be recognized as His domain. This implies a new worldview, where the workplace becomes a sacred space and seeking the welfare of the community becomes a spiritual activity.

3. Missional vs. Attractional—The church does not exist for itself, like some holy country club, but to affect the world. We don't want to just attract a crowd; we must intentionally equip people. This means we need to replace our feel-good sermons with instruction that prepares and mobilizes people to go out and do the mission of transforming Babylon. Now training and equipping must feed into mobilization and commissioning engagement where people feel and believe they are sent on mission.

Back to the story of Jesus feeding the five thousand: when the little food they'd begun with had been distributed to all those groups of fifties and hundreds, there were twelve baskets full of leftovers. It was a true miracle.

Have you ever wondered what happened to those twelve baskets? I have. I like to think they were taken somewhere else to bless other regions. That's what city changers are when they exit the doors of the church. They are great blessings to those inside the church, but then they spill out to bless the spheres of the culture of Babylon.

Three Stages of Spiritual Maturity

When it comes to producing city changers through our discipleship processes, is it possible to measure spiritual growth? I think it is, and John lays it out in his first epistle:

I write to you, little children,

> Because your sins are forgiven you for His
> name's sake.

I write to you, fathers,

> Because you have known Him who is from
> the beginning.

I write to you, young men,

> Because you have overcome the wicked one.

I write to you, little children,

> Because you have known the Father.

I have written to you, fathers,

> Because you have known Him who is from
> the beginning.

I have written to you, young men,

> Because you are strong, and the word of God
> abides in you,
> And you have overcome the wicked one. (1
> John 2:12–14)

John describes three levels of spiritual maturity: children, young men, and fathers.

I don't believe he's referring to natural children, actual young men, and older men who are fathers. I believe he is writing to *spiritual* children, spiritual young men, and spiritual fathers, especially since he gives his reasons for calling them by those titles.

He calls one group children because their sins are forgiven. They are just beginning the spiritual journey, having recently received forgiveness for their sins. The cross has redeemed them from guilt and shame. This is in essence how we enter the kingdom of God—we embrace the privilege of knowing that our sins are forgiven.

When a physical child is born, everything in that household changes. The noise levels change; the sleeping patterns change; the size of the car changes; the time it takes to go anywhere changes. Everything changes to accommodate the new child. When the baby starts crying, both parents rush to assist. Everything seems to revolve around the child.

The same is true spiritually. When people are born into the family of God, they are spiritual babies and they need attention. It is so important that spiritually mature people are willing to go down to their level, so to speak, to connect with them and assist in their growth process.

When a baby crawls around on the floor, his parents have to keep an eye on him because anything he picks up is likely going straight into his mouth. It is the same spiritually. Spiritual babies think they can "eat" anything. Young Christians are susceptible to some very weird ideas because they cannot yet distinguish between what is healthy spiritual sustenance and what is not.

Plus, some unhealthy content seems preferable to what's better for us. If young children must choose between pizza and vegetables, we all know what their choice will be! Their parents must guide them to eat what is healthy and good for their growth. Our challenge is to have enough spiritual parents to guide the spiritual children into the full stature of Christ.

John also addresses young men. (Please understand that John is including women in his entire discussion here. As all are referred to as the bride of Christ, so all are called young men.) He says that defining characteristics of a young man are that he is *strong*, has the *Word abiding in him*, and *has overcome the evil one*.

He is talking about people who are no longer children but have matured into a position of strength. There is something about the Word that defines them now. Their decisions are guided by it.

I think John means that spiritual young men have been able to withstand challenges and temptations. We are not talking about perfection but rather about beginning to have more victories than defeats.

This person is growing and maturing. When a child is small and cries, the parents run to help. But when that child is eighteen and still cries for attention, Mom and Dad may tell him or her to grow up! Spiritual children must also grow and mature. They must stop crying and start taking responsibility if they wish to become spiritual young men and women. We must refuse to accommodate spiritual babies who have been on the journey for many years; we should instead expect people to be growing to the full stature of Christ.

But there is a risk in becoming strong: there is a tendency to move from dependence to independence. When you have experienced victories in your spiritual life, you might begin to think you don't need anybody anymore. You might think you are strong enough to function on your own. This is when many people isolate themselves from the body of Christ in the local church.

Your challenge now is to move to the next level of maturity: a spiritual father.

A spiritual father has matured to the point that he is ready and willing to begin helping the next generation along. He takes responsibility for helping spiritual children become spiritual young men, and he works with spiritual young men to make them spiritual fathers themselves.

John's whole idea is to reproduce a spiritually mature family cycle, where there are always children, young men, and fathers. This is God's model for discipleship.

To move someone through those spiritual phases, we must disciple people to *know God, love people, and impact their world.* The spiritual father then becomes a mentor to spiritual children to develop them through these three areas, growing them into spiritual young men.

The Discipleship Process

What does it look like, in practical terms, to raise children to become young men? Do you have a discipleship framework within which you will know when you are strong, the Word of God abides in you, and you have overcome the evil one? In the discipleship process, we suggest there are three focus areas:

1. Knowing God—stirring a passion for your identity in Christ, intimacy with God, and integrity in life
2. Loving people—stirring a passion for compassion toward others, discovering your calling and how to invest your resources
3. Impacting your world—stirring a passion for the evident presence of Christ in your neighborhood, your community, your city, and the nations of the world

Discipleship in essence is a journey of discovery. God starts His work in you at salvation, and you discover the privilege of knowing Him. This is discovering what God is doing in and for you. As you grow, you come to discover that God wants to work not only *in* you but also *through* you. The love of Christ will start touching people's lives through you. This leads to the realization that God is on a mission here on Earth and we have the privilege of sharing in His agenda. Then you discover that living out your purpose and calling will affect the world, allowing His kingdom to come.

This is how believers enter their destinies and become city changers who step out to transform Babylon.

Let's look at each of these three areas.

Knowing God

In discipling people to know God, there are three important points of emphasis, which we looked at in the chapter on the accomplished work of Christ. They are:

1. Identification with Christ
2. Intimacy with God
3. Integrity in life

For us to truly disciple people to know God, we need them to see that Jesus's victory on the cross is their victory too. It's a victory you and I had no role in yet we claim identification with.

First, those we disciple must understand that we died with Christ. Now, you and I weren't really there. But we were spiritually there, and sin's power over our lives was officially broken as we died and were buried with Him (see Rom. 6:4).

Secondly, we were also raised with Christ into resurrection life. The power of the flesh can never create the fruit of the Spirit. True discipleship leads believers to discover their inclusion in Jesus's victory and teaches them how to live out of that reality. Identity precedes activity.

Thirdly, we are seated with Christ in a place of authority (see Eph. 2:6). Because He suffered and died on the cross, we are no longer fallen people but are once again welcome as people resident in God's chambers. We are now seated with Him in heavenly places where we rule and reign with Christ. Obviously, you and I are still living here on Earth. But in our identity, we are already raised, victorious, and coreigning with Christ.

The first step in knowing God is *identifying with Christ* in His death, His resurrection, and His current reign.

The second step in knowing God is entering into *intimacy with God*. The growing disciple needs to understand that God has made His residence in him. On the eve of His death, Jesus said, "In that day you will know that I am in my Father, and you in me, and I in you" (John 14:20 ESV).

People live differently when they realize the Creator God is in them. God lives *in* us—so we ought to live as those who are connected to Him. The connection I'm speaking of is not some inferior acquaintance with a transcendent God who lowers Himself to our level. Rather, it is the glorious reality of God raising us to His level and transforming us into His image to enjoy glorious union with

Him. I can no longer think of myself in isolation. I am no longer an individual, separated from God—I am in union with Him.

We will transform Babylon only if we understand our *identity* in Christ and our *intimacy* with God.

The third aspect of knowing God is achieving *integrity in life*.

In Ephesians, we read about three actions the Christian undertakes.

1. First, we *sit* with Him in heavenly places (see Eph. 2:6).
2. Then we *walk* in a manner worthy of our calling (see Eph. 4:1).
3. Finally, when we have done these, we *stand* (see Eph. 6:11).

We tend to think that if we *walk* well, God will allow us to *sit* in heavenly places. But it's the other way around. It all starts with the way we sit. If you sit well, you will walk well. If you know who you are, it will change the way you live. We are not trying to adjust people's behavior; we are teaching believers who they truly are in Christ, because knowing who you are in Christ will affect your behavior.

Some time ago, one of my colleagues went to the doctor because he was having back pain. When the doctor asked him to turn around, he saw that my friend had a large wallet in his back pocket. He asked him whether he always carried it there, and my friend said he did. The doctor told him the pain in his back was further aggravated by him sitting incorrectly as he compensated for the wallet in his pocket. Because he sat incorrectly, it affected the way he stood and walked. This is a spiritual truth too. If we sit wrong, we'll stand and walk wrong. We must sit correctly!

To know God, we must identify with Him, have intimacy with Him, and live in integrity.

Recently we were on safari in South Africa, traveling in a Land Rover that had no side doors. We encountered lions in the wild. One of the big male lions approached the vehicle, and in that moment of vulnerability, I became aware of the incredible authority this beast carried. He was not intimidated by our large vehicle.

I've also seen lions in the circus, where the animal seems anxious, running around in the arena very aware of a man cracking a whip. That lion does certain tricks to the applause of the people, but it has not internalized that behavior. When the lion goes back to its cage, it does not continue to practice the tricks. Why? Because there is no whip. We must be cautious not to define integrity as adjusted behavior on the basis of anxiety and fear of punishment, but we must rather recognize it as the outcome of our discovery of who we truly are.

Once we are established in knowing God, we take the journey of living beyond ourselves, where we become an instrument of grace to others.

Loving People

God not only wants to work in you, but He also wants to work *through* you. In order to do that, you must

- be motivated by *compassion*.

- live out your *calling*.
- understand your *contribution*.

Compassion is a motivation of love.

Many people view love as a feeling. But love is actually a value statement. When you value something, it evokes positive emotions. When you devalue something, your emotions toward it become negative.

God puts *value* on every human—even the ones we'd rather not have anything to do with. Every human being is the carrier of the image and likeness of God and therefore has value. If we can gain God's perspective of every living person, it will change the way we look at them and value them and therefore how we engage with them.

God bought us at the cost of His Son. Talk about a king's ransom. What you are willing to pay for something depends on the value you place on it. You're willing to pay more for a car than for a phone and more for a house than for a car. Why? Because of the perceived value of that particular item.

Why did we cost so much? Why did God have to pay for us with the life of Jesus? Why was He willing to spend the life of His own Son to purchase us? Because He was redeeming the very image and likeness of God in humanity. There was logic in His love. God saw in humanity enough value that He was prepared to pay the very blood of His Son.

> You were not redeemed with corruptible things, like silver or gold, from your aimless conduct received by tradition from your fathers, but with the precious blood of Christ, as of a lamb without blemish and without spot. (1 Pet. 1:18–19)

Loving people requires that you have compassion for them motivated by seeing people as God sees them.

Loving people also requires an understanding of *your calling,* the idea that every believer is called to ministry. Calling is not just the privilege of an elect few. By virtue of being a believer, you automatically qualify to be called.

For some people, no matter how long they wait or how hard they search, the elusive "calling" never becomes clear. They look with envy at people living out their calling and ask—what's wrong with me that I don't know what I'm supposed to do with my life? Why does He have something unique for them but not for me?

In the Bible, God does indeed call people to particular work, but more often than not it is not specific. He does, however, give all people broad guidance for their work. The point is that God has given everyone the ability to recognize something the world needs. He seems to expect us to notice it and get to work rather than wait for a special call from Him. There is no biblical formula for translating the needs of the world into a precise calling. The single strongest indicator of what God wants you to do is probably your awareness of what needs to get done to make the world more like what God intends. This doesn't necessarily mean huge, global problems but simply anything in the world that needs to be done.

If you want guidance for how you can most significantly play a role in God's bigger plan, try quieting yourself and answering the following questions, which may help you uncover your passion:

- What do you love doing with your time?
- What activity gives you energy?

- What do you want to change, shape, and leave
  better in the world than you found it?

A love for people is motivated by compassion and fueled by your calling. But we are also entrusted with the things we have to steward as our *contribution* to the plan of God on Earth. This contribution is measured by how you steward your life.

God has given us finances, time, and personal gifts we could use for His purposes. We don't own those resources, but we are their temporary managers or stewards. The Bible says we will one day appear before God and give account of how we lived.

> We must all appear before the judgment seat of
> Christ, so that each of us may receive what is due
> us for the things done while in the body, whether
> good or bad. (2 Cor. 5:10 NIV)

God wants to work not only in you but also through you, and one way He does so is when you love people.

Impacting Your World

The third focus of discipleship is becoming a city changer: transforming Babylon. There are three aspects to this:

1. Embracing a new *worldview*—where Christ is
   Lord of all

2. Recognizing the *workplace* as sacred and a place
of ministry

3. Seeking the *welfare* of the community where
you live

First, city changers need the correct *worldview*. Believers must discover that Jesus Christ is Lord of all. That understanding will change how they survey the horizon. They need to grasp that the kingdom of God entails every square inch of the cosmos. All spheres of life fall within the Lord's jurisdiction. Jesus is Lord of education. He is Lord of business. He is Lord of the government. He is Lord of the media. He is Lord of the arts. He is Lord of all. Everything comes into perspective when we recognize His lordship.

To affect their world, city changers must also know how to function effectively in the *workplace*. They must discover that their workplaces are their places of ministry. Every Christ follower is called. Some, those in professional ministry, will live out their calling by serving the local church. But most believers will seek to obey their calling out in Babylon. They will serve their Lord in the context of their everyday work and life.

Sometimes businesspeople wrongly think that since they aren't professional clergy, they aren't doing anything to serve the Lord. They may feel guilty and thus obligated to serve at the church—teaching or handing out bulletins on Sunday mornings. But during the week they are working in schools or doing service jobs or even heading up companies through which they are blessing the whole community. Now, I'm all in favor of Christians using their gifts to build up the local church. But if you have a job out in the streets of Babylon, that is your primary calling.

The dualistic split between "sacred" and "secular" must be abandoned. The things of the workplace are spiritual—just as spiritual as church and worship. I am living out my spiritual life not only in Jerusalem but also in Babylon.

Finally, city changers must work for the *welfare* of Babylon. Many Christ followers ask, "How do I engage a godless culture? How do I enter this space dominated by resistance to the Light?" But even framing the questions that way is a precursor to defeat. We're operating from a position of authority and victory, after all.

Believers need to know how to engage this world as faithful and fruitful agents and how to trust God for wisdom and power. Christians must grow from spiritual children into spiritual young men and women, but they must also become spiritual fathers and mothers.

This graphic depicts the process of discipleship we use in Doxa Deo to raise city changers:

8

TRANSFORMING TOGETHER

In a vision this big, we all need help. No one church or ministry, no matter how large, can make a dent in the *lostness, pain,* and *brokenness* of the region on their own.

That's not how we like to think. In churches—and I don't mean large churches only—we tend to want to concentrate on what we can do. Sometimes we can even come to believe that our church or our ministry is the only one out there doing good.

But if we become aware of the extent to which our communities have been damaged, we realize that this is a job bigger than any of us. We start asking new questions: questions about how we could have greater impact and how we could bring more good to bear on the problems.

If the church is going to positively affect and even transform Babylon, we're going to need to make a fundamental paradigm shift in how we approach ministry.

A paradigm is a framework of assumptions. True community transformation will not succeed if all we do is add programs to our existing paradigm. What we've been doing in church ministry up to now has been good, but it isn't big enough. Much of the church's engagement in the community in the past has focused on *benevolence,* not really on transformation. By transformation, we mean shifting the needle in the spiritual, social, and cultural dimensions of our cities. Transformation will not happen unless we harness the collective capacity of the kingdom in the regions we serve.

Among pastors, there is a growing realization that their local churches cannot do the job alone. However, they have often been frustrated in their attempts to come together in a concerted effort. There is great pressure on them from within to make their own churches a success. So many leaders are on the verge of burnout, many times comparing their situations with the perceived successes of ministries around them. Many of them don't understand how to take care of their own souls, so the last thing they want to do is add another obligation, especially one not focused on their own church's needs.

The tendency I see in many unity movements is shared *activity* without shared *goals or outcomes.* Churches might be willing to work together in a show of church-to-church bridge building—and that's a good thing—but it's only so much busywork if they're not consciously working toward the same goals and outcomes. This can take a very positive desire to transform disintegrating cities and turn it into more frustration and exhaustion.

What will it take to create a prolonged and sustainable unity movement within the church that will transform whole regions for the kingdom?

Lessons from Florida

I've seen just such a movement firsthand. May you take insights from this story and be inspired to apply it to your own situation.

Ironically, it all started when some prominent churches in the South Florida region of the United States experienced major challenges and embarrassment. A few key churches lost their senior leaders in less than desirable circumstances, and this caused a crisis.

It was within this context that I was approached by some friends in the Florida region, asking whether I would spend a few months coming alongside one of the newly appointed leaders of a megachurch in the region. The church had more than twenty thousand members, but it was functioning in an insular way as opposed to cooperating with other ministries in the area.

With a few exceptions, this inward focus was shared by every church from Miami to Palm Beach. In this region of approximately 5.5 million people, Barna Research recognized only 4 percent as being fully committed Jesus followers.

I initially agreed to three months of support for this new leader. My mandate was to come alongside him in this new and complex responsibility of leading a local megachurch. It was clear from the outset, however, that he knew he had to lead that church into a new season. He especially wanted them to join hands with other ministries in the region. This emphasis sparked an exciting new movement of collaboration within the whole county.

Several churches in the region gained new pastors during this time—young, humble, and magnanimous leaders. They created a new sense of hope and anticipation that a new season had dawned, and this sparked a fresh desire to reach across denominational and other divides. In the providence of God, most of the seasoned leaders who had already been faithfully serving in this region also came on board, which lent credibility to this process.

I wonder whether it was the painful and embarrassing situations these young leaders inherited that caused them to reach out to one another in a new and fresh way? They were asking the question "How can we represent the kingdom in this region better than our predecessors did and in a unified way?" Perhaps we can say that crisis created opportunity. You have probably heard the saying "Never waste a good crisis."

I found myself in the midst of leaders who wanted to collaborate in order to bless and affect their communities. I saw that God was moving supernaturally to bring key leaders together in a new sense of mission, and this stirred my heart. We moved our global Doxa Deo headquarters to South Florida so I could be closer to what was happening. I feel blessed to have been called on to help design the process going forward.

The Church United

The collaborative dialogue expanded across three counties: Miami-Dade, Broward, and Palm Beach. Early on, two megachurches in the area and two large nonprofit organizations committed to forming and financially supporting an office dedicated to this united effort for at least three years.

We established a process called Church United, in which we can facilitate engagement among churches and ministries on three levels, represented by the terms *connect, collaborate,* and *celebrate.*

1. Connect—creating unity—facilitate opportunities for leaders to discover, dialogue, and do life and outreach together.

2. Collaborate—catalyzing action—identify spiritual, social, and cultural goals that can be reached more effectively together.

3. Celebrate—cultivating transformation—measure the positive outcomes of these efforts on the culture and the region.

We are discovering that for collaborative ministry to work, leaders must reformat the way they approach ministry. There is a need to embrace a series of paradigm shifts. We must change the value systems that drive our ministries.

To maximize our impact on our communities, as church leaders and members we need to make the following shifts:

- *From concern to compassion.* "When Jesus landed and saw a large crowd, he had compassion on them" (Mark 6:34 NIV). The disciples were driven by concern, but Jesus was driven by compassion. Concern sees the problem but feels overwhelmed and wants to send it away, hoping that someone else will take care of it. Compassion, on the other hand, gets engaged, trusting that God will reveal Himself and provide what we need.

- *From condemning your city to seeking the peace and prosperity of it.* "Seek the peace and prosperity of the city to which I have carried you into exile. Pray to the LORD for it, because if it prospers, you too will prosper" (Jer. 29:7 NIV). For too long, we as the church have positioned ourselves as adversaries of our communities. We must realize that what we're actually called to do is serve, engage, and bless our cities. Eventually we get the city we deserve.

- *From building walls to building bridges.* "You are the salt of the earth.... You are the light of the world" (Matt. 5:13–14 NIV). When it comes to how the church stands in relation to our communities, we must realize that God has made us salt and light. We cannot remain outside the community, inviting people in. We must go out to our communities and immerse ourselves in our world in order to make a difference.

- *From measuring attendance to measuring impact.* "The kingdom of heaven is like yeast ... mixed into ... flour until it [has been] worked all through the dough" (Matt. 13:33 NIV). The question "How big is your church?" should be replaced with "What impact and influence does your church have in your community?" Or better yet, with this question: "If your church ceased to exist, would the community feel it as a loss in any way?" We need a new measuring focus as well as new measuring instruments. You cannot measure temperature with a ruler. If we have the wrong instruments, we will get the wrong feedback. By counting only "nickels and noses," we will never be able to quantify missional impact.

- *From encouraging to equipping.* "[Ministers are] to equip [Christ's] people for works of service" (Eph. 4:12 NIV). In our churches, many members feel that "ministry" and "calling" are things restricted to the professional clergy. All Christians need to be aware that they are called to ministry in the context where God has placed them in their daily functioning, and we as the church are called to consider how to equip and empower them to represent the kingdom well in those spaces.

- *From local minister to regional spiritual leader.* "As [Jesus] approached Jerusalem and saw the city, he wept over it" (Luke 19:41 NIV). We must understand that our responsibility as spiritual leaders does not end with our local congregations. Like Adam, who was placed by God in the garden of Eden, we, too, have been placed in a city or geographical area, and we need to take responsibility for it. A lost and broken community needs spiritual leaders who will initiate change in those areas.

- *From positioning against to joining hands.* "[May] they all ... be one, as You, Father, are in Me, and

I in You" (John 17:21) and "Two are better than one because they have a good reward for their efforts" (Eccles. 4:9 HCSB). Joining hands with others—forming strategic alliances for greater impact—involves a vision for kingdom goals, a servant attitude, generosity of spirit, and a desire for unity. Though various denominations may have differences in theology, ecclesiology, and methodology, those who embrace an orthodox perspective of Scripture can all agree on the gospel and celebrate whenever it is declared across Babylon.

- *From shared activity to shared goals or outcomes.* "I chose you and appointed you that you should go and bear fruit, and that your fruit should remain" (John 15:16). When we want to make a difference, our tendency is to gravitate toward activities, not outcomes. So we find ourselves doing many things together but not really evaluating whether they contribute to sustainable change or transformation in the region. But when we start thinking of outcomes, we define what we want to change and then align all our activities to serve that particular goal, which can be measured and evaluated.

Defining shared outcomes empowers collaborative action by the churches in communities. Collaborative sharing in mission does not require congregations to make long-term organizational commitments to one another but rather to the shared outcome. Each church can determine its contributions and activities within the framework of its own unique convictions. Although the approach to actions might differ, all are working together to achieve the same outcome. Collaborative mission does not require everyone to be pressed into the same theological, methodological, or ecclesiastical mold. Rather, this collaboration is unity behind one purpose: the common desire to make Jesus Christ known to the whole community as Savior, Restorer, and Lord. When we commit to bringing faith, love, and hope to a community, unity becomes our collaborative vehicle.

We believe this might be what Jesus was praying for:

> My prayer is not for them alone. I pray also for those who will believe in me through their message, *that all of them may be one,* Father, just as you are in me and I am in you. May they also be in us so that the world may believe that you have sent me. I have given them the glory that you gave me, *that they may be one as we are one*—I in them and you in me—so that they may be brought to complete unity. *Then the world will know* that you sent me and have loved them even as you have loved me. (John 17:20–23 NIV)

Vision and Strategy

Although we are still in the early stages of the Church United process in Florida, we have seen exciting collaboration throughout the Tri-County area. Working on the three concepts of *connect, collaborate,* and *celebrate*, greater unity and shared goals have emerged and are being embraced and expressed in different ways across South Florida.

There is within the Church United platform a group of key leaders from the region who help convene other leaders and mobilize their churches into greater involvement in society. We have engaged in these action steps that have been helpful in the process:

- Researching the region and sharing information—assessing spiritual, social, and cultural needs and building an asset map of what is already being done through the church.
- Showcasing regional and global best practices and highlighting specialist practitioners.
- Facilitating interministerial/intermissional dialogue forums to encourage engagement and synergy to achieve the determined outcomes.
- Hosting regional gatherings of leaders, facilitating impartation and dialogue, creating unity, and bringing clarity and alignment to the vision.
- Catalyzing action in the arenas of spiritual, social, and cultural transformation.
- Inspiring Christian marketplace leaders and societal activists to come alongside the process.
- Celebrating the progress of societal engagement and transformation through web-based and public platforms. One such early victory for us was when we had to contend with the crisis following a shooting at the Fort Lauderdale airport. This gave

the church the opportunity to rise to the moment and serve in a significant way. The churches working collectively were able to give $68,000 toward medical bills and other needs of the victims.

In order for your own collective church movement to be successful, you must have a strategy, which consists of vision and mission. We created one at Church United that might serve as a starting point for the strategy you create with your team.

> **Vision:** Unifying and mobilizing the church to bring *faith, hope,* and *love* to all of South Florida.
> **Mission:** Unifying and inspiring leaders to *connect, collaborate,* and *celebrate.*

When we had our vision and our mission, we understood that this strategy automatically represented a threefold challenge to the church leaders involved. They must understand these so they can rally around the outcomes they desire.

The threefold challenge to leaders is this:

> 1. A spiritual challenge: own the *lostness* of your region. Estimate the number or percentage of fully committed Jesus followers in your region and see how you can grow this group through the collective efforts of the church.
> 2. A social challenge: own the *pain* of your region. In what ways are people hurting in your area?

Those can be the issues you target. For South Florida, the breakdown of healthy relationships and the unique social pain of every subregion became the primary focus.

3. A cultural challenge: own the *brokenness* of your region. What are the things that are broken in your area? Here we contend with institutional components of society that define the way we do life. These constitute the cultural dynamic of the region. Education. The government. The justice system. Business. Arts and media. What do these areas represent, and what causes misalignment with kingdom life and brings pain to the city? Your cooperative church alliance should ask these questions and focus on those needs.

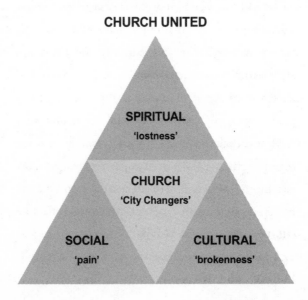

CHURCH UNITED

SPIRITUAL
'lostness'

CHURCH
'City Changers'

SOCIAL
'pain'

CULTURAL
'brokenness'

From Strategy to Tactics

Up to now, I've been speaking of things any church alliance can do in its area. But you'll be breaking these strategic initiatives down into actionable goals and tactical plans. The specifics I list below are what we've decided to do in South Florida. Your plans may look very different from these, and that's perfectly fine. I just want you to see one way of translating big-picture strategy into small-picture action points.

In South Florida, here's how we translated our threefold challenge into tactics for pursuing the outcomes we desire:

> 1. We want a good spiritual outcome. Our practical goal: focus on spiritual outreach to the region to see a specific percentage increase in Christ followers whom Barna would consider evangelical, or as mentioned, "fully committed Jesus followers." We have determined the baseline, and we ask every region to determine its own goal in this regard.
>
> 2. We want a good social outcome. Our practical goal: focus on the breakdown of family and relational health in the region so that selected societal trends are addressed collectively in different regions. Here we can measure the divorce rate, struggling single-parent-led families, juvenile delinquency and incarceration, and foster care and orphan engagement, which are all related to the breakdown of the family structure.

3. We want a good cultural outcome. Our practical goal: focus on education as the key to securing the future for the next generation so that failing schools are turned around and literacy levels rise in the region.

The exciting part is that this is not just a South Florida phenomenon. We are seeing this sort of cooperation all over the globe. What we experienced in Pretoria, South Africa, for over twenty years, where leaders reached out to one another to ask how we could make a tangible difference in the quality of life in our communities, we are now experiencing in regions across the world. We are personally involved in the same dialogue in other regions of South Africa, Australia, Europe, South America, and the United States. We are also aware that God is sharing the same sense of missional engagement in many other nations in the world.

Many unity movements celebrate at most a bit of collaborative prayer, and maybe some spiritual/social engagement. Very few entertain the idea of cultural transformation. We must move from feel-good joint events to a vision of the church coming together to transform Babylon.

The mission of Christ includes the personal restoration of every individual and extends to the restoration of all created things.

9

UNDERSTANDING OUR CULTURAL REALITY

Unity with fellow churches is wonderful. But true unity is possible only when all parties understand that Jesus, in His glorious act of redemption, was reconciling *all things* to Himself.

Personal salvation is part of this, but not all of it. Jesus also redeemed our world. He is Lord of all, and that includes all created reality.

So long as we think that only people are covered under redemption, we won't work as hard for the good of this world. We'll be inclined to hide away from the world and let people sort things out for themselves. If we are to share in His mission, we need to embrace His full intentions for His act of redemption.

This is why spiritual leaders should feel obligated to take responsibility for transformation within our communities. Our villages, towns, and cities need to become spaces that reflect outwardly the same redemption we have experienced in our personal lives.

A village, town, or city is first *people*. Second, it is a *place* to express communal life, concentrate opportunities, steward resources, and exercise good governance. Cities have personalities and even spiritual characteristics of their own. We must function with discernment to identify what the areas of celebration and brokenness are in our communities. We do this so we can attempt to make Christ preeminent in all aspects of society.

We have a responsibility to serve the city in which God has placed us. Our engagement in our communities means taking the responsibility to invest in its prosperity, steward its resources, be purveyors of peace, and proclaim the life of Christ over individuals and corporate society. That's how righteousness, peace, and justice can prevail so we can bring the aroma of Christ to our cities.

All Mission Begins with God's Initiative

God was there from before the beginning of all we know and perceive. And God continues to be everywhere. As in, *everywhere*. Psalm 139:8 suggests that even if you make your bed in hades, you will find God there.

God is already at work in any spot we might visit in the world. In situations of utmost despair and suffering, of crime, corruption, and chaos, God is already there. Our job is to recognize God's presence and discover how He is working. The secret is not to pray for God to "do something" in those situations but to recognize what He is already doing and align our efforts with His initiative.

In redemption, God always takes the initiative. This is true in personal salvation as well as cosmic redemption. We align our efforts with what God is already making manifest. Any mission we might pursue on Earth must therefore be the result of God's initiative and must be rooted in God's ongoing purposes to heal all creation.

God's Desire Is to See Restoration, Reconciliation, and Redemption in All Things

The New Testament focuses on *restoration, reconciliation,* and *redemption.* God's agenda is to be present in creation, and His presence makes the world a place of shalom, of completeness, wholeness, health, welfare, safety, soundness, tranquility, prosperity, perfection, fullness, rest, and harmony. The earth is to be a place of love, forgiveness, justice, security, well-being, blessing, and salvation.

God is manifesting the kingdom not only in heaven but also right here on Earth. And you and I have the glorious privilege of being invited into this activity.

We don't have to plead with God for His kingdom to be expressed on Earth as it is in heaven. Rather, it's we who need to become burdened with God's purpose for this era in history.

Throughout Scripture and history, we have seen men and women become burdened with God's intent. They aligned themselves with that purpose in such a way that they could be used by God to change the course of history and affect the destiny of nations.

One such person was Nehemiah.

He became an instrument of grace to restore not only the broken walls of Jerusalem but also the lives of the people who lived there.

In that way, Nehemiah joined God's plan to position the Jews to effectively receive restoration.

Nehemiah demonstrated what it's like to make the presence of God felt in a community. This needs to be understood on three levels, which we can call *the presence framework*:

1. The Fathering Presence—a burdened heart—an *awareness* of the need of Christ's presence in the world
2. The Faithful Presence—a bended knee—the *aroma* of Christ in the world
3. The Fruitful Presence—a busy hand—the *action* of Christ in the world

As I said early on, we all want to live in communities that are blessed, functional spaces where we can truly flourish. As God's people, we desire communities that reflect His glory. However, our actual situation rarely matches our preferred situation. We often don't live in godly environments, and more often than not, we as the church end up standing in condemnation of our city. Or we enjoy the offerings of the city but don't take into account the underlying challenges of the city, and we stand aloof from any engagement.

We're overlooking that the church has a fundamental contribution to make to the quality of life of our communities. If we're standing apart from our city so we can condemn it, it's partially our fault that we get the community that we deserve. It's the reality we helped create, albeit through passivity.

God has given the local church—and the church universal—the mandate of engaging its community in such a way that men will see

His glory manifested in every sphere of society. As God's ambassadors on Earth, we must be present (mixed right in with) the communities where we live. If we are to transform Babylon, we'd better be walking its streets and taking its pulse as citizens, neighbors, and leaders.

Let's look at how the presence framework was expressed in Nehemiah's life.

The Fathering Presence

We must recognize there is a difference between burdens that are right for us to bear and burdens that are wrong. We should never bear the burden of sin or doubt, but there are some burdens placed on us by God, which He does not intend to lift from us until we respond and engage in making a difference. God will burden us to make a difference in things within society that are negatively affecting the people in the community.

We can engage Babylon by caring about its people. If you're bringing a message of change but your attitude and actions reveal that you don't really care for the people you're offering it to, not many are likely to want what you're selling. But if you demonstrate a burdened heart for the people and their hurts, the situation will be different. If you actually care for them as people and families, not to judge them or preach to them but to love them as fellow sojourners, they'll be more likely to want what you've got. This is how we become God's presence within the world.

Nehemiah was deeply aware of the need for God's presence in the world. For him, it all started when he became divinely burdened by the condition of Jerusalem.

Likewise, if we are to be city changers, we, too, must be deeply stirred over the terrible absence of the presence of Christ in our communities. Because when you are burdened by something, the first thing that happens is that you develop a growing *awareness* of the challenge it represents.

It's completely possible to live within a very broken environment yet be totally unaware of it. We can become so engrossed in our little world that we are ignorant of the problems around us—and completely blind to what God may actually want to do about them through us.

Sometimes God wants to take us beyond our comfort zone.

Yes, Nehemiah had been a Jewish slave in Babylon. Not exactly what we might think of as anyone's definition of a comfort zone. But he really did have it posh, especially compared with his countrymen. He was working for the king *in the palace* and enjoying all the attendant privileges and benefits. Babylon was a highly developed city, with paved roads and, of course, the Hanging Gardens, one of the seven wonders of the ancient world.

Further, Nehemiah had probably never been to Jerusalem. He had only heard about it. If you had to be an exile and a slave, Nehemiah was positioned in the best spot to endure it. Certainly, if he were in Jerusalem, he wouldn't have it so easy. Jerusalem was a shantytown compared with Babylon, at least at that time. If Nehemiah had done what many people would've advised, he would've just lived out his days in comfort and privilege.

But God got hold of his heart, and suddenly Nehemiah became *burdened*. He heard a report about conditions in Jerusalem, and he felt overwhelmed with the need to do something about it.

> I asked [the messengers who had come from Jerusalem] concerning the Jews who had escaped, who had survived the captivity, and concerning Jerusalem. And they said to me, "The survivors who are left from the captivity in the province are there in great distress and reproach. The wall of Jerusalem is also broken down, and its gates are burned with fire."
>
> So it was, when I heard these words, that I sat down and wept, and mourned for many days; I was fasting and praying before the God of heaven. (Neh. 1:2–4)

Nehemiah became aware of the problem, and it created a sense of responsibility, a burning burden, which is the prerequisite for expressing God's fathering presence in a community. If he had closed his ears to the report from the messengers, he could've gone on blissfully ignoring all things concerning Jerusalem and its people.

In your community, go out *noticing*. But beware, because once you understand the need around you, you may become compelled to do something about it.

Barriers Nehemiah Had to Overcome

Once Nehemiah decided he wanted to do something about this burden he'd developed for Jerusalem, a host of obstacles came to his mind:

- He'd been born in Babylon and had never been to Jerusalem. By the time of Nehemiah, the Jews had been in captivity for more than one hundred years. Everything he knew about Jerusalem had been told to him.

- The journey to Jerusalem was approximately nine hundred miles and would require about four months of travel. How was he going to make that happen? Not only would it be a massive undertaking, but he also wasn't exactly a free man able to go on holiday whenever he liked.

- There was the legitimate fear of bandits and criminals on the way.

- He was uncertain about what sort of reception he would receive in Jerusalem, if he somehow gained permission to go there and crossed the miles unharmed.

- Speaking of which, he had no idea how he was going to gain the king's permission to be released from duty. Nehemiah wasn't just some random slave the king would never miss. He was the king's cupbearer, which was an important and trusted position. Despots weren't in the habit of doing without the people they found useful.

- Nehemiah even felt a spiritual responsibility for the way things were in Jerusalem, though he'd never even seen the place. He prayed, "[I] confess the sins of the children of Israel which we have sinned against You. Both my father's house and I have sinned. We have acted very corruptly

against You, and have not kept the command-
ments, the statutes, nor the ordinances which
You commanded Your servant Moses" (Neh.
1:6–7).

- He would have to leave the comfort of Babylon,
the most developed city in the known world. He
would be exchanging the palace for the desert
wilderness and his bed for hard ground.

If you let them, the problems you identify when you gain a
burden for a community can make you feel defeated before you do
anything. Don't let them! Nehemiah felt that his burden was from
God, and that meant God wanted him to do something about it …
and would *enable* him to do something about it, despite the many
obstacles in the way.

Like a loving parent kneeling in prayer for a child, let your burden and awareness mix with faith in Christ, and He will make you
a fathering presence in your community. Sometimes we are on a roll
in our lives where everything feels as if it's going really well and flowing effortlessly. Then we sense the challenge to embrace something
new—something out of the norm of our everyday lives. As we stretch
a little out of our comfort zone, we come across obstacles where we
didn't expect them to be, and they even become roadblocks in the
way of us reaching our desires. This is where we need to know that
we embraced the vision, not on the basis of convenience but because
of conviction. It is this conviction that defines our fathering presence
in a region. We take responsibility for the burden beyond our need
for comfort and convenience.

The Faithful Presence

Christians are called to be not only a fathering presence in Babylon but also a faithful presence. We are to be salt and light, the very aroma of Christ in the world. We transform our culture with bended knee. Our spirituality needs to be presented, not in a false and posturing way but in an attractive way that causes people to desire the love, acceptance, and grace we show.

Nehemiah was clearly a man of action. He managed to get permission to leave the king's service for this project. He even managed to get the king to fund the trip and furnish the supplies they'd need. Then, when Nehemiah actually got to Jerusalem, under his command the wall was completed in only fifty-two days. But he was not just a man of action—it is clear he was also a deeply spiritual man.

Nehemiah did not stop praying. There are at least ten references to his prayer life in the book, more than most any other leader in Scripture. He was keenly aware of his need for God, though he felt secure as a leader.

Likewise, prayer and humility form the bedrock of transformation movements, which become the foundation for community transformation.

Prayer

Prayer has been the central element to every spiritual awakening in history. Every great move of God in cities and nations in the past was birthed by prayer and was sustained by the persistent intercession of Christ followers.

We should not underestimate the impact of the prayer that happens when church leaders and the body of Christ bind their hearts together in supplication before God in bold proclamation over the regions they take responsibility for.

When leaders gather to pray, it is a demonstration of our utter dependence on God. We rely on Him to empower us beyond what we are capable of accomplishing on our own. In any unity process in a city, consistent corporate prayer must take place. Also, be sure to create moments of public intercession when the body of Christ can ask for more of His power and glory to be revealed in the community.

In the Tri-County area of South Florida, the leaders of our unity movement have dedicated the first Wednesday of every month to prayer and fasting. This is when all the churches relating to Church United give expression to prayer. They do so in their various ecclesiastical traditions, but they do so knowing they are in solidarity with one another in bringing the region before God.

Of course, we know prayer does not persuade God to do things He was not already inclined to do. We're not twisting God's arm. But we also know that, through prayer, we align ourselves with His desires. Through our petitioning and proclamation, we invite heaven to invade Earth. Scripture is clear that we have not because we do not ask (see James 4:2). May we never forget that.

Humility

Few traits are as important in leaders and those in the unity process as humility. Few things are as beautiful to see as humble leaders reaching out to honor, revere, and celebrate God's grace in one another's lives and ministries.

> Make me truly happy by agreeing wholeheartedly with each other, loving one another, and working together with one mind and purpose.
>
> Don't be selfish; don't try to impress others. Be humble, thinking of others as better than yourselves. Don't look out only for your own interests, but take an interest in others, too.
>
> You must have the same attitude that Christ Jesus had. (Phil. 2:2–5 NLT)

God opposes the proud and gives grace to the humble (see James 4:6). That's not just something that finds expression individually. It's also true at the corporate scale of a city or a geographical region. When leaders demonstrate humility, they usher the grace of God into their city.

Isaiah reminds us that God chooses to associate Himself, not with the proud and the lofty but with those whose hearts are humble before one another and before Him.

> Heaven is My throne,
> And earth is My footstool.
> Where is the house that you will build Me?
> And where is the place of My rest?
> For all those things My hand has made....
> But on this one will I look:

On him who is poor and of a contrite spirit,

And who trembles at My word. (Isa. 66:1–2)

Bring a bended knee to your city, in prayer and humility, and you and your unity movement will become the faithful presence in Babylon.

When Christ sent the disciples out on their first recorded mission, He said He was sending them as *"lambs among wolves"* (Luke 10:3). I have often wondered what this meant. If I had been one of the twelve disciples, I might have put up my hand and asked, "Jesus, can't we rather go as wolves among lambs? It just feels as though we then would have more influence."

But Jesus was adamant about the "lambs among wolves" principle. And as we find ourselves in Babylon, we realize that we represent a new kingdom. We must live out our kingdom values in an environment that is dominated by a different value system.

In Babylon, we are definitely lambs in the midst of wolves. Yet Christ supplies us with power to overcome each wolf and thrive in a wolf-dominated culture. This is what it means to be a faithful presence in our spheres:

- Hate we counter with love.
- Indifference we counter with compassion.
- Pride we counter with humility.
- Greed we counter with generosity.
- Resentment we counter with forgiveness.
- Abuse we counter with empowerment.
- Manipulation we counter with serving.

Many Christians encounter a "flesh" action and react with a "flesh" response. That's the most natural way to act, of course. But doing so will cause us to miss the opportunity to be a faithful presence in that moment. The fleshly response makes us no different, in that moment, from non-Christians and aligns us with the same spirit that is governing Babylon. We have to enter into self-centered "ego-systems" and present them with kingdom ecosystems.

The Christian response is to overcome evil with good. Where there is pride, we want to come with humility. Where there is resentment, we come with forgiveness. This is how we operate in the power of the opposite spirit. Operating with this attitude makes you feel weak—sort of like a lamb surrounded by wolves. But Paul reminds us that when we are weak, God makes us strong (see 2 Cor. 12:10).

We have to be aware of the spirit with which we are engaging our world. We need this awareness at all times, not just when we are confronted with opposing forces that we can immediately identify as being the ungodly representation of Babylon. We must be equally sensitive to which kingdom we are representing, even when we attempt to do good.

Much has been written about something called "toxic charity." This happens when people who are relatively wealthy or empowered give money or other resources to solve an immediate need for the poor or disempowered.

An example of this might be an annual event in which the rich dare to drive into a poor neighborhood, drop off a gift or meal to pretty much anyone poor, and drive out again as quickly as possible.

What could be wrong with that? The givers feel they have done a good thing, and surely the recipients are benefited. And if they understand that the benefactors did their deed in the name of Christ, doesn't everyone win?

The reality is that what drives this initiative is oftentimes the ego-need of the givers. They may be motivated by a need to feel better about themselves rather than the desire to truly help transform the circumstances of the receiver. The problem is that it doesn't give the recipients a chance to rise above their circumstances. Indeed, such acts of toxic charity can even contribute to worsening poverty and encouraging an attitude of entitlement.

Nor is it spiritually healthy for those doing the toxic giving. The relatively wealthy often do such deeds with a sense of superiority and in a patronizing way, thinking they are representing the kingdom well by giving of their excess to those who need. The reality is that much of this activity contributes to a wolf attitude and does not position them as kingdom lambs.

If we wish to be a faithful presence in Babylon, we must understand the calling we have as lambs. Believers representing the kingdom of God will often stand in contradiction to the desires of the flesh. We do desire to influence all spheres of society, but not in the fleshly sense of wanting to conquer them. We must not be driven by a desire for power, pride, or control. We must keep ego in check. We're here to transform Babylon, not become its new kings and queens. Nor are we here to step into roles of influence with the wrong spirit or with a few pet scriptures we feel endorse our triumphant engagement. We're ushering in a new way of living through surrendered lives, and we do so in all the places where we live, give, serve, play, and pray.

Christians are indebted to the mercies of God. Since we have been so wonderfully treated by Him, we are called to adopt a lifestyle of serving others. As inheritors of the New Testament, we are instructed to give higher priority to the needs of others than to our own (see Phil. 2:4).

Paul reminded the Corinthian church that Christians are to always look for opportunities to bless, not for what benefits we ourselves have the "right" to receive. He says that he seeks to please others in everything he does, not seeking his own advantage (see 1 Cor. 10:33). If people see our good works, it may prompt them to realize their need for God. That's the power of sacrificial, loving conduct, because of how countercultural it is and how different it is from what most people do.

Being a faithful presence in the sphere of your daily work means so much more than being on time and not stealing paper clips. It means more than giving vague gratitude to God for a good bottom line in your company. You now represent a totally different way of life. How you represent the gospel is what can make it attractive to all. Paul says we should behave "so that in every way [we] will make the teaching about God our Savior attractive" (Titus 2:10 NIV).

The Fruitful Presence

If you want your Babylon to be transformed, you're going to have to roll up your sleeves and get a little dirty. A busy hand, extended for the good of your community, becomes the very action of Christ in the world.

Nehemiah was a man of action, as we have seen. And yet, after learning of the need in Jerusalem, Nehemiah isolated himself before taking any overt action. He took four months to wait on the Lord and formulate his plans.

Nehemiah's Strategy

After his designs were ready, he pursued them, and God gave him success. Notice these things about his strategy:

He took calculated risks. Especially when he stood before the king to lay it all out.

> And it came to pass in the month of Nisan, in the twentieth year of King Artaxerxes, when wine was before him, that I took the wine and gave it to the king. Now I had never been sad in his presence before. Therefore the king said to me, "Why is your face sad, since you are not sick? This is nothing but sorrow of heart."
>
> So I became dreadfully afraid, and said to the king, "May the king live forever! Why should my face not be sad, when the city, the place of my fathers' tombs, lies waste, and its gates are burned with fire?" (Neh. 2:1–3)

Note that he spoke to the king while the queen was with him and that he spoke to the king *after* he had served him generous portions of wine. His timing was calculated and effective.

He anticipated possible problems:

Furthermore I said to the king, "If it pleases the king, let letters be given to me for the governors of the region beyond the River, that they must permit me to pass through till I come to Judah." (Neh. 2:7)

He did research and planned the engagement well:

"And [please give me] a letter to Asaph the keeper of the king's forest, that he must give me timber to make beams for the gates of the citadel which pertains to the temple, for the city wall, and for the house that I will occupy." And the king granted them to me according to the good hand of my God upon me. (Neh. 2:8)

Nehemiah's Communication

He communicated his vision clearly. When he spoke to his fellow Jews in Babylon, he said:

You see the distress that we are in, how Jerusalem lies waste, and its gates are burned with fire. Come and let us build the wall of Jerusalem, that we may no longer be a reproach. (Neh. 2:17)

You also need to be able to communicate your vision for a transformed community to the people who can join you in the effort.

Nehemiah's Organization

Read Nehemiah 3 and pay attention to phrases such as "next to him" and "next to them." That idea appears thirty-one times in thirty-two verses. Nehemiah had the ability to organize people and coordinate their efforts. That's a skill you will need as well.

His organizational scheme was simple and therefore effective.

> Then Eliashib the high priest rose up with his brethren the priests and built the Sheep Gate; they consecrated it and hung its doors. They built as far as the Tower of the Hundred, and consecrated it, then as far as the Tower of Hananel. Next to Eliashib the men of Jericho built. And next to them Zaccur the son of Imri built.
>
> Also the sons of Hassenaah built the Fish Gate; they laid its beams and hung its doors with its bolts and bars. And next to them Meremoth the son of Urijah, the son of Koz, made repairs. Next to them Meshullam the son of Berechiah, the son of Meshezabel, made repairs. Next to them Zadok the son of Baana made repairs. (Neh. 3:1–4)

He worked with people who wanted to work.

> The next section was repaired by the men of Tekoa, but *their nobles would not put their shoulders to the work under their supervisors.* (Neh. 3:5 NIV)

It's a losing proposition to try to get people to work who don't want to be there. They'll be slack in their work, they'll stop as soon as your eye is off them, and they'll bring down the morale of everyone around them.

Nehemiah gave ownership to everybody and delegated responsibilities. Everyone had a role to play. He mobilized as many as he could.

We pursue a fruitful presence in the spheres of society when we ask how we can influence the system in which we're involved. How can I ...

- engage education with kingdom values?
- engage business with kingdom values?
- engage government with kingdom values?
- engage media with kingdom values?
- engage the arts with kingdom values?
- engage sports with kingdom values?
- engage social services with kingdom values?
- engage the church with kingdom values?

Christ followers must ask this question about every sphere of society in which they're involved, whether it be the arts, media, sports, social services, or even the church.

We want people to be mobilized into all spheres of society. They do so by having a fathering presence, a faithful presence, and a fruitful presence in Babylon. This is how we will start the process of transforming our communities. We need to mobilize individuals in their engagement with the spheres of society as kingdom agents.

After mobilizing individuals, we step up to the next part of the strategy, which we refer to as *engagement,* which is of a more corporate nature.

10

ENGAGEMENT

Here we affect the spheres of society at the corporate level with a plan and a strategy directed toward outcomes within the various spheres.

Here we map out the existing institutions in our community and ask how we can better engage them with kingdom presence. Let's consider a few spheres of our society.

Local Government

One of the best places to start is to ask how you can engage the local governmental authorities. Many evangelicals feel their local authorities are hostile to Christians. But that perception isn't always reality.

For a unity movement to be effective, it must seek partnerships with other role players in the community. Formal community institutions and local government councils who need to partner with the local community will, as a rule, gladly join hands with a unified expression of the church.

Many city and county governments are reducing their social spending. So if civic authorities are to survive, they must find creative ways to partner with the community and outsource as much as possible. This may present an opportunity for the church to move in and increase its services to fill that vacuum. Here the church has an advantage because, unlike other organizations, it relies less on grant funding and more on the generosity of its members.

When we consider entering into a partnership with a civic organization, we need to think of it as a long-term relationship. This should not be limited to a single church's relationship with someone they might know at the city council level. It should be broader than that.

It is helpful if the authorities have one phone number to ring and one group to deal with when they engage the Christian community. The solution we've come up with in South Florida is to create an office that represents all the churches working together. This is so much easier for the city officials than if they have to call up several churches when they need something done.

Not only is it smart to do things as a unified group, but it also bears witness to the gospel when we are in *unity* when we engage our comm*unity*.

It always goes a long way with the local authorities when we contact them, not to get something from them but to ask how we as the Christian community can serve the agenda they are implementing in the city. Most everyone else goes to them wanting help. They don't expect someone to do the opposite. We do well to ask them what their key priorities are for the community they are serving. It really excites them when you ask how your group of churches can help them reach those goals.

Of course, your coalition may not be able to meet all the needs that are presented. But just think of the impact you could have on that local authority's opinion of Christianity if you could actually meet one or more of them? Remember, we are here to seek the welfare of Babylon.

> Seek the welfare of the city where I have sent you into exile, and pray to the LORD on its behalf; for in its welfare you will have welfare. (Jer. 29:7 NASB)

We are here to be a blessing to the place God has called us—not to place a further drain on it. We will not only gain respect and support from our local authorities if we contribute to their goals but also usher in God's plan of restoration to all creation. Actually, the local authority functions as an extension of God's intention for our world.

> Let every soul be subject to the governing authorities. For there is no authority except from God, and the authorities that exist are appointed by God. (Rom. 13:1)

Education

Much of the low-hanging fruit for engagement within communities is within the area of education, but educational environments often feel out of reach for the Christian community. There are laws that govern this and some good reasons for the separation of church and state. However, that doesn't mean Christians shouldn't affect the sphere of education. The distance between Christ followers and a secular humanistic educational environment has been made to seem wider than it should or could be.

There are so many wonderful examples, in both the developed and the developing worlds, of Christian teachers showing up at their schools with a heart to serve and a love for these environments, and this has resulted in large inroads for kingdom life. Wouldn't it be incredible if, in every city and town, each educational institution had a church dedicated to praying and interceding for it on a weekly basis? Think of the impact such a thing could have—and to do it, we don't even need permission.

We have the opportunity to reach out to pray, serve, and engage the educational entities of our communities. We can spread the light and love of Jesus in that environment just by being present.

Think about the schools in your community. How could your church come closer to those schools? In what ways could your group reach out to the headmasters or principals, teachers, coaches, parents, and students? In many cases, doors will open for us to be involved so long as what we're doing is not deemed overtly religious. We could bridge that gap and be right in those corridors of learning, demonstrating kingdom life in a way that could cause many to search for Christ.

What's more, many schools are open to after-school activities where churches or ministries can openly invite people to discover life in Jesus Christ.

I believe it is counterproductive to position the church as an adversary of public schools. How much better to come alongside them as partner and champion.

It's not only adults from a church who can influence a school. Christian students themselves ought to be encouraged to excel in school because of their own sense of calling. Plus, they must desire to achieve in order to qualify to attend the best universities and colleges they can. In this way, we are teaching our children how to take the lead in culture and society.

Daniel's story in the Bible is helpful for us in this regard. He and his young Jewish friends were forced to receive some of their education within a very pagan environment. Just as Daniel and his friends were raised within a Babylonian culture and ultimately transformed it, so we take up the challenge to achieve positions of influence to deeply affect our Babylon.

This dedication to learning, despite the unrighteous system they found themselves in, spoke well of them and caused them to be put into key leadership roles in the kingdom.

> Then the king ordered Ashpenaz, chief of his court officials, to bring into the king's service some of the Israelites from the royal family and the nobility—young men without any physical defect, handsome, showing aptitude for every kind of learning, well informed, quick to understand, and qualified to serve in the king's palace. He was to teach them the language and literature of the Babylonians. (Dan. 1:3–4 NIV)

Notice some of their qualifications: a good appearance, *an aptitude for every kind of learning, being well informed,* and *being*

qualified to serve in the king's palace. Because of their approach
to learning, they were seen as being fit to play roles within the
context of a very secular environment. The king's own advisers
handpicked these boys for the highest political positions in the
kingdom.

Daniel and his friends were trained in an educational system that was foreign to their Hebrew convictions, but somehow
they were not intimidated. Their biblical worldview became the
lens through which they interpreted the culture in which they
were immersed. This is key to how we can engage an educational
system that might seem hostile toward our Christian beliefs and
convictions.

Sometimes that system actually *is* hostile toward Christianity.
Daniel continues to be our example. He didn't compromise his convictions but consistently did what he knew was right.

> The chief official gave them new names: to Daniel,
> the name Belteshazzar; to Hananiah, Shadrach;
> to Mishael, Meshach; and to Azariah, Abednego.
> But Daniel resolved not to defile himself with
> the royal food and wine, and he asked the chief
> official for permission not to defile himself this
> way. (Dan. 1:7–8 NIV)

Daniel did not protest, nor did he insult the culture of the
Chaldeans. Rather, he engaged it with resolute grace. He accepted
their culture but did not compromise his convictions. He allowed
himself to be renamed but stood firm in his true identity.

This should be such an inspiration for our young Christian students today. It actually is possible to function *in* the world without being *of* the world.

> In all matters of wisdom and understanding about
> which the king examined them, he found them ten
> times better than all the magicians and astrologers
> who were in all his realm. (Dan. 1:20)

Daniel and his friends were blessed by God and granted favor in their journey. We, too, can enter into that blessing. In Christ, we live with a sense of calling, favor, and destiny that sometimes translates into huge moments of divine opportunity and tangible blessing.

God calls us to be present in our culture's educational system. We must not withdraw from it, because that would be to surrender the next generation to humanism and godlessness. God doesn't call us to turn our backs on any of the spheres of society but to transform them. And you don't transform something you're not part of.

The Arts

I love what our good friends Roger and Lesley Sutton from Manchester have achieved by engaging the arts community of their city. Lesley shares her journey:

> In the summer of 2012, whilst on retreat, I sensed
> God speaking to me about using my passion and
> training in art as a means to share His love for the

people of Manchester, the city where I had lived for the past 25 years. Gradually, I began to form a picture of an arts trail across the city centre during the season of Lent that would explore themes taken from the Passion narrative using a variety of art forms, including sculpture, painting, contemporary installation, and sound. I felt it was important to restore the festival of Lent within our city's cultural calendar, as it has much to offer contemporary society as a seasonal space in which to pause, reflect mindfully, and learn to live more simply and compassionately amidst the stresses and activities of everyday city life.

PassionArt was formed after many meetings and conversations. We partnered with six significant cultural spaces in the city centre, three sacred and three secular, from the cathedral to the City Art Gallery and Museum, and invited both internationally renowned and local artists to exhibit works that explore themes of existential meaning: belonging, guilt, fear, loss, suffering, love, mercy, hope, and resurrection. These bi-annual art trails are marketed as contemporary pilgrimages, spiritual exercises that all can explore, religious or secular, either as a single reflection in a lunch hour or as a full day's pilgrimage.

Each work of art is accompanied by a written reflection and a practical response in our carefully crafted art catalogue. This helps participants engage spiritually and practically with the themes and thereby interact with their spirituality in a non-threatening and self-led manner.

The PassionArt Trails open on Ash Wednesday, beginning with an event at the cathedral that includes live music, artist talks, curatorial reflections, and wine and nibbles. Key people from across the city are invited to join us and further live events accompany the trail at our other host venues. The city art museum worked with us to host a number of lunchtime led reflections around the selected artworks in their spaces. An evening of live improvised music, curator tours, and mindful drawing classes were hosted by venues to join with the cities "late night" creative programmes.

As we dismantled the artworks at the end of our eight-week 2016 PassionArt Trail, entitled "Be Still," we were pleased that, according to our host venues statistics, their visitor numbers had increased by between 10,000 and 15,000 during our Lenten art festival. Thousands of our art catalogues, with their reflections and prayers, had been taken by the visitors, and we were invited to speak on national BBC radio as well as local stations on a number of occasions.

Responses at each of our art trails has been overwhelmingly moving. Visitor books, e-mails, and newspaper and journal articles expose how viewers responded and related to the themes the art raises. Here are two examples:

"To engage not just with our spiritual 'side' but indeed with the spiritual beings we all are through this trail was incredibly special indeed."

"To be able to discuss why death is terrifying, why cancer doesn't override or devalue the entirety of our humanity, and how deep beauty can be seen within our brokenness, the asylum seeker—refugee or not—cannot help but stir that 'Other' longing within us all. To have the space to do this, though, is not a lifeline many of us regularly give ourselves the gift of."

We are learning together how the arts can be used to have an impact on our towns and cities, the communities where we live and serve amongst. Artists act as agents of social and cultural change, and as the church we have lots to learn from them.

The role of the artist, in my mind, is to inspire a poetic and dangerous imagination that sees the world as it is, depicting the pain, suffering, death, and anxiety we all experience in the fallen state of the present moment as well as the paradox of the beauty within the suffering and wounding. But the artist is also called to depict the world as it could be, as it will be when the Kingdom of heaven comes in all its fullness, through the seed of hope and truth present within the beauty and ordinariness of the present moment.

We need to help culture imagine a different consciousness by refusing to fully embrace the all-consuming, apathetic numbness that too often dominates our towns and cities. We need to create art that imagines an alternative way of living with and embracing paradox that acknowledges, expresses, and creates symbols for the deep suffering that is our experience, whilst looking towards the healing of the nations.

The artist's temperament is gifted to hear the cry of Creation, the pain of humanity, and to help us to feel and empathise with our inherent condition in a fallen world.[11]

Business

Similarly, my friend Risco Balenke from Holland engaged his business, motivated by kingdom principle. Here is his story:

Individualism, self-employment, self-determination and self-realization have become more and more important in Western society. The promises of the French revolution still remain: Liberty, Equality and Brotherhood. But the greatest of these are Liberty and, of course, Equality. However, "Some pigs are more equal than others," and that's where the Brotherhood ends.

For decades, we have intertwined our democratic freedom with a capitalistic view on the marketplace. And yes, for a long time, this brought our Anglo-American society ever-increasing wealth.

Meanwhile, capitalism transformed into neo-liberalism, bringing an increasing supremacy of liberalization, economics and capital. These days less than ten people own more wealth than half the world's population combined. And history shows that elites, obtaining sufficient economic and political power, tend to enrich themselves at the expense of the many.[12]

In everyday life, this often means that to secure financial profit or share value for the rich, workers will be dismissed or given temporary contracts. They juggle multiple low-wage jobs, leaving them less able to take care of themselves and their families. This inequality creates new patterns of subjection. Workers are no slaves, but neither are they free. This applies to individual people as much as it does to regions of the world.

All this is a far cry from the biblical principles of stewardship and the Year of Jubilee (see Lev. 25:8–55). Stewardship comes with responsibility and care for people and planet. The Year of Jubilee served to expel inequality caused by any reason whatsoever.

Our Christian worldview inspires us to care for the weak and the poor, the widow, the orphan and the stranger. Charity as a virtue is highly valued, and rightly so! However, I have discovered that, especially in the area of business and economics, justice is a more important virtue.

In Micah 6:8 we are called to bring justice. And exactly this wake-up call is addressed to the city, the marketplace, to apply fair and just principles in business.

This is my main worry, my sincere question: How culturally conformed are we in our conviction that the shareholder has the legal right to make decisions about the company, holding the sole legal claim on the profit? Why do we think it normal that the owner of a company can sell it for his own benefit—leaving the employees the burden of earning back the price the new owner paid, usually by suffering cost-cutting reorganizations and layoffs? Whose capital is really at risk here? Do we really have a deep understanding of the effects of joblessness and poverty in families? Do we really care?

I rarely hear Christian entrepreneurs questioning these principles, let alone wondering about the idea that employees could have rights in decision making or profit sharing. I'm not denying generosity in shareholder charity. I'm questioning the justice in regarding this as charity! How can we relate stewardship and the Year of Jubilee to the call from Micah?

There is another way. A way in which the supplier of financial capital is compensated with interest and the supplier of human capital is compensated with salary. These suppliers take part in joint decision making, as both have long-term interest in the well-being of the company. They share profits because profits are generated in successful cooperation between financial and human capital.

For almost fourteen years I was the CEO of a €230 million, fifteen-hundred-employee company in the Netherlands. We worked this way. This company applies the principle of stewardship: shareholders do not see the company as their property. This opens the way for rethinking and *redesigning* the position of shareholders and other stakeholders. How miraculous, seeing shareholders happily sharing decision making with employees just as they share profits: fifty-fifty! This sharing is no charity but a just obligation. By doing so, shareholders lowered inequality as prescribed by the Jubilee Principle. By leaving profits in the company, they built the necessary financial resilience to overcome economic downturns without laying off workers—a new version of the Joseph Principle: filling the granaries in the good years to be able to feed the people in the bad years (instead of sending them out of the country in times of famine)!

Even more surprisingly, shareholders and employees both accepted lower profit rates so disabled people with a distance from the labor market could work with us. While lowering efficiency rates and profit margins, we gained dignity and an inclusive culture. We applied the principle of not harvesting the corners of our field, as mentioned in Leviticus 19:9, to take care of the vulnerable—those who, without support and protection, wouldn't have income. Again, that's no charity but a God-given instruction, as if He knew we probably wouldn't do it voluntarily.

So my call is this: How can we rethink our business assumptions? Jesus was in many ways countercultural. We need Ezras for the temple and Nehemiahs for the city. Who dares to ask disruptive questions to challenge the current culture in Babylon?

I saw civil servants crying, hearing about possibilities for disabled people to get jobs. A Dutch political party leader included the story of our company in his book *It Is Possible*.

It's not about two ends of the line: either capitalism or socialism. It is about us cracking that line and creating a God-given new dimension. It is about rethinking stewardship and the Year of Jubilee, about bringing justice in the marketplace, not as charity but in a structural way: in *organizational design*. It is about changing the fundamental architecture of our economy. Let us challenge ourselves with new creativity to let these principles come true! To love one another as brothers and to really set everybody free—because to God we are equal!

We as the church need to engage our culture right where it is. If the schools are not coming to the church, the church has to go to the schools, or the arts, or business, or any other sphere of society. If we don't like Babylon, we must change it. But education, business, government, media, the arts, and the other spheres won't change until we show up!

11

THE GENEROSITY PRINCIPLE

There is something glorious about discovering the selfless life.

Christians are called to live beyond themselves, to have someone other than themselves as the center of their affections and actions. We will truly influence our communities only when we put the interests of others before our own.

It is only when we embrace a posture of selflessness, of *generosity,* that we bring the redemptive nature of the kingdom to our communities. We can extend God's grace to a broken world only when we choose a sacrificial life. This is simply choosing to live as Jesus did. Our Lord lived generously, one day at a time, in all He thought and did.

I like the way the Amplified Bible (classic edition) says it. Note that the italics, parentheses, and brackets are in the text of the Amplified Bible. They're not my additions.

> For you are becoming progressively acquainted with
> *and* recognizing more strongly *and* clearly the grace
> of our Lord Jesus Christ (His kindness, His gracious
> generosity, His undeserved favor and spiritual bless-
> ing), [in] that though He was [so very] rich, yet for
> your sakes He became [so very] poor, in order that
> by His poverty you might become enriched (abun-
> dantly supplied). (2 Cor. 8:9 AMP)

Did you notice the phrase "His gracious generosity"?

Generosity spreads an amazing ripple effect out into the world. When we are generous, it touches our families and our communities and our workplaces. Its effects are immeasurable.

Jesus asks us to live generously. The Gospels show our Lord challenging some folks to make drastic changes in their lives or to give away all they had. To the confusion of the disciples, Jesus challenged a rich man to sell everything he had and give it to the poor (see Matt. 19:21). After Jesus's resurrection and return to heaven, the early church in Jerusalem decided to generously share what they each had so that no one would be without. The Bible even says they "had everything in common" (Acts 2:44 NIV). (However, this might not imply they shared everything to the fullest extent and retained nothing in private ownership. The emphasis is on their generosity to their fellow believers.) Now, that was pretty radical.

Sometimes we will be challenged to make great sacrifices for the sake of the kingdom. But the generosity I'm speaking of consists of small, everyday deeds of love, compassion, and blessing. Sometimes the small act of generosity feels harder than the big, one-off gift.

When benefiting others in our communities becomes part of our lifestyle and when we're open to the generous life, we're beginning to transform our culture.

We need to live lives that cause the world to wonder why we love and serve so well. If every Christ follower practiced this kind of generosity, we would see a great spiritual awakening take place in our neighborhoods, towns, and cities across the world.

> Be wise in the way you act toward outsiders; make
> the most of every opportunity. (Col. 4:5 NIV)

Evangelism that is effective today is not *proclamation* alone but proclamation plus deeds of *demonstration*. This is living out the love of Christ, when ordinary believers devote themselves to consistent sacrificial acts of kindness and choose to love their enemies and forgive those who persecute them (see Matt. 5:44). That does sound a little like what Jesus was saying, right?

This feels very modern, but it's actually not unique to our times. The early church made inroads into the Roman Empire, not through grand moments of public proclamation but through sacrificial service in the marginalized sectors of society. Their influence grew so effectively that, in the fourth century, Emperor Julian feared Christians had become so strong as to pose a threat to the Roman Empire.

Julian noted how generous the Christians were, and he felt he needed to institute a government-led social program to do the same thing. It was recorded as a miserable failure, as most social programs are, because it was not driven by the heartfelt compassion that motivated the Christ followers in the empire.

This, I believe, was the spirit behind Paul's admonition to those who were in slavery at that time:

> Exhort bondservants to be obedient to their own masters, to be well pleasing in all things, not answering back, not pilfering, but showing all good fidelity, that they may adorn the doctrine of God our Savior in all things. (Titus 2:9–10)

Paul wasn't condoning slavery. He was saying that if Christians *are* slaves, even then they could practice generosity that might lead to making the gospel attractive.

In the same way, you and I can make the message of Christ attractive as we practice acts of generosity. Not on rare occasions only, but consistently through everyone in the church. We need to mobilize all followers of Jesus to foster generous living as a part of their missional calling. In every church we need to teach this, create opportunities to practice this, and celebrate the times we see it in action. In Doxa Deo, we ask people to share their stories with us so that we can publicly celebrate them, because as we've mentioned, what you celebrate you will replicate. Consistent small random acts of kindness create a culture of generosity in a community.

We now live as people who, as a consequence of God's reign in our lives, desire to be generous. The desire to be hospitable, available, and encouraging to everyone around us wells up inside. Generosity has a way of surprising people. It is countercultural, but it's also contagious. When someone is truly generous, it affects both the giver and the recipient, and it leaves both sides different from how they were.

I'm often amazed by the genius of the words of Jesus. Generosity—the principle underlying "Love your neighbor as yourself" (Matt. 22:39)—sums it all up. Jesus didn't say that loving your neighbors would be easy; He only said it would work. It would be a contribution to move them toward faith in God. Generosity toward those around us was one of God's best ideas.

Can you imagine what would happen if Christians became known for their unquenchable generosity? Picture the major shift in communities all across a city or a region when Christians consistently share words of affirmation, do random acts of kindness, offer prayer and small tokens of appreciation to all who work with or live around them. Can you see it?

People outside the church don't usually think of generosity as a defining characteristic of Christian people. (Sad, isn't it?) Instead, they think Christians sit in judgment, bound by rules and obligations that suck the joy out of life—or worse: Christians just want money. This is why even skeptics are caught off guard when they encounter generosity from people who freely share what they have and who do this because they are Christians.

I know of several ministries that grew out of some small deed of generosity. You never know when that act of kindness you have in your heart might bloom into a major initiative that blesses multitudes.

Breaking Off Small Pieces

The story of Jesus feeding the five thousand reveals a principle of generosity that starts with taking small steps.

Jesus told the disciples to have the large crowd sit down in groups of fifties and hundreds. Then He blessed the bread and fish and began breaking the bread into smaller chunks. But the miracle hadn't become evident yet. He didn't break the bread out in a big show of multiplication, resulting in barrels and barrels of bread all around His feet. That would've made the disciples feel secure, because then they would've seen that the reserve might actually match the need.

Instead, Jesus broke the bread into just a couple of parts and put it in the hands of the disciples.

I can just see those disciples ... looking at the bread ... then looking at Jesus ... looking at the people ... looking at the bread again and realizing they might have a riot on their hands.

I imagine one of the disciples going to a group of a hundred with his piece of bread but deciding to start with a group of fifty instead, where the risk seems lower. I see him breaking off the first piece. I'm sure it must have been a small piece. He's smart, and he knows that this tiny bit of bread in his hands must last.

Can you imagine the guy who got the first piece? "Wait, this is *it*?"

And the disciple answers, "Well, yes ..."

The disciple breaks a piece off for the next man and then yet another piece. But as he does, he realizes that something strange is happening in his own hands. The more he keeps breaking and sharing it, the more there is to give away!

So often we are faced with the same challenge. We feel we don't have enough to give, or we think we don't have the resources or capacity to meet the need. When that happens, we need to apply the same principle our hapless disciple used: just start breaking off small pieces.

In the early years of Doxa Deo, some of the police officers in our church came to ask whether I knew exactly how bad our city really was. They offered to escort me and a few of our leaders into the inner city of Pretoria at midnight on a Friday evening.

We arrived at the police station, where they gave us insight into the vices of the city. They then took us to those places. As we were traveling to different spots, I happened to see hundreds of people on the pavement sleeping on newspapers and flattened cardboard boxes. I asked the policeman who these people were and what they were doing.

"They sleep here every night," he said.

"But why," I asked, with kind of an attitude, "do you allow it?"

He looked at me sadly. "They have nowhere else to go."

That statement rocked my world. I was deeply shocked. I hadn't even known there were people so desperate in "my" city. I lived out in a leafy suburb and never went to the inner city, certainly not at midnight. Awareness brought the need to my attention, and the burden was born. I wondered what other needs there might be in our city that I wasn't aware of.

Before going on this nighttime journey, I told the church I was going to do so. Therefore, they expected my report. I remember making this statement the next Sunday as I was preaching: "I plead with us as the church, before we get all hung up about the sin of our city, let's do something about the pain of our city."

A few days later, somebody came to my office with two homeless people in tow. He asked me what we were going to do with them!

"I don't know," I said. "Why did you bring them to me?"

"Because you told us to do something about the pain in the city."

I realized then how easy it is to talk—and even to preach—about making a difference but how hard it is to actually do it.

So there I stood with my church member and two homeless people. I knew we had to just … do something. So we lined up a place for them to stay.

Whew! I thought the crisis was over. But when word got out about what we'd done, people started bringing more of the homeless to us! Soon we had a full-blown situation on our hands, and I realized God had to help us.

It came to our attention that there was a big three-story building in our city that was empty and dilapidated. It was on the "wrong" side of the city, and nobody wanted to go there. But it was the only building we could find. It was in terrible condition. It had no windowpanes intact, the water was not working, and the lights and electrical wiring had all been stolen. But, hey, it was a building—with a roof.

I stood before the church and said, "I have exciting news: we've found a building! It's in a bad area, but now at least we have something to work with." I said I'd need help to fix the building.

Some of the people just looked at me. "Alan, it's in a dangerous area, but you want us to go work there?"

Nevertheless, I found a few people who were willing to help, and we got the building fixed up enough that we could allow people to live in it.

I soon realized we'd made a big mistake! By giving the homeless people a place to stay, we had just brought all the related problems together in one building. We had all kinds of challenges that we had no knowledge of how to address. About the only people we pleased were the drug dealers, who were happy because now all their customers were under one roof!

But this was all part of our journey that taught us to trust God by breaking off small pieces that would result in an incredible miracle.

We quickly discovered we needed to get these people out of our building and back to being economically active. But we didn't know how to do it.

So then we thought, *Hey, let's start a recycling business and ask everybody to bring their trash. Then these people can sort everything and sell the trash.* But it was terrible! The trash came pouring in, but—surprise, surprise—it was challenging to sort, and it stunk! This wasn't working.

Of course, we were able to do this because it was a bad area of the city that did not get much attention from the authorities, and in the process, we were probably violating a few of the local health codes. Today we laugh when we think about how we went about so much of this, but we also realize that even in the midst of what could be deemed a chaotic picture, God was with us.

Soon we realized that many of the people were ill and needed medical attention. We arranged for doctors and nurses to come and serve. At least we weren't a garbage dump anymore. As this developed into a more efficient and effective outreach to the people who were in residence, people in the surrounding community decided they wanted to come for medical help too. It was inevitable that we should establish a medical clinic, which led to the opening of a dental clinic and then to the opening of an eye clinic.

The focus was always on the homeless we had in the building. We wanted to teach them valuable skills and then help them find jobs. To facilitate this, we partnered with a company to get their applications out to various companies. We even developed an entrepreneurial training program to help individuals set up their own small businesses.

As of this writing, we have approximately eighteen vocational skills being trained at various times of the year. We train for jobs in hospitality, home-based care, basic office administration, arts and crafts, as well as more advanced skills such as construction, carpentry, and forklift driving.

Perhaps the greatest outcome of all this is that the city took notice that the Christian community was serving the disempowered of the city in a very tangible way.

I'm so proud of what has come about through this. Now, in partnership with a research company and the University of Pretoria, we track the effect of this investment by monitoring the transformational impact on individuals, their workplaces, and their immediate communities.

Roughly one thousand people go through our People Upliftment Program (we call it POPUP) every year. Fully 70 percent of the people who have gone through our program have been placed back into the mainstream economy, where they feel a new sense of dignity and are able to sustain not only themselves but also, in many cases, family and friends around them.

Here's an even better 70 percent number: 70 percent accept Jesus Christ as Savior and Lord while going through the program. The testimonies they write are riveting. These people open up about moving from desperation, brokenness, and a sense of hopelessness to an embrace of a new life of hope and joy in Jesus Christ.

What started out as us reaching out to a few homeless people, in a very uncertain way, has now developed into a premier skills training institution and the most effective outreach evangelism program of our ministry.

It started by us *breaking off small pieces*. Initially we didn't have the answers, and we didn't understand how to do everything, but we responded to what we sensed God was saying to us, and look what happened.

The pathway to a life of generosity is strewn with little pieces of bread broken off in faith and offered to those in need.

12

THE GENEROSITY PARADIGM

I believe there are two kinds of people on the earth: *givers* and *takers*.

At its core, being a Christ follower means you go from being a taker to being a giver. In all the relationships we navigate, our lives need to be marked by giving, not getting. This is what Christ modeled for us.

> Husbands, go all out in your love for your wives,
> exactly as Christ did for the church—a love marked
> by giving, not getting. (Eph. 5:25 THE MESSAGE)

There is hardly any element of Jesus's life, including the deeds He did and the stories He told, that does not illustrate some facet of generosity. Jesus was constantly showing the blessing of living in a spacious, generous way.

And remember the words of the Lord Jesus, that
He said, "It is more blessed to give than to receive."
(Acts 20:35)

The Gospels depict Jesus as consistently giving—many times
to those who could not reciprocate the blessing. He gave freely of
His time to children, to the marginalized, and to women, who were
greatly devalued in that era. He kept company with Samaritans, and
then told of their generosity, to challenge the status quo. He gave
dignity to those who were rejected by the establishment of the day:
the lepers, the blind, and the lame.

Jesus identified four attitudes in people: two kinds of takers and
two kinds of givers.

> Takers
> > Wolves
> > Goats
>
> Givers
> > Sheep
> > Lambs

Wolves

Wolves are takers. Their motto is "What's yours is mine, and I'm going
to take it." These people are consumed with greed. Wherever this was
evident, Jesus was quick to address it, especially where it manifested in
those who were supposed to represent the religious leadership of the day.

> You Pharisees make the outside of the cup and dish
> clean, but your inward part is full of *greed* and wick-
> edness. (Luke 11:39)

Jesus was warning the people about those who only pretended to be righteous. Unfortunately, many of them were people of influence in that day. Perhaps you've heard the term "a wolf in sheep's clothing." Well, that came from Jesus:

> Beware of false prophets, who come to you in
> sheep's clothing, but inwardly they are ravenous
> wolves. (Matt. 7:15)

Greed is an insatiable longing for wealth, status, and power. It is an inordinate desire to acquire or possess more than one needs. At its root lies pride and discontentment, which cause a person to strive for more and care less about others.

Consumerism becomes excessive—becomes *greed*—when it causes us to strive to attain more only for the sake of fulfilling our own hedonistic desires or to live without any sense of being a blessing to others. And when the culture around us makes excessive consumption appear normal, any of us can become a ravenous wolf.

Of course, it is important to say that we're not speaking against wealth per se. We're talking about greed. Wealth in itself can be a great blessing if it is in the hands of a generous person. The issue is not that we have stuff. It becomes an issue when the stuff has us.

Some people behave in greedy ways because of serious psychological dysfunctions. If they feel a deep sense of inner emptiness or worthlessness, they can seek to heap up possessions and wealth in an effort to salve that inner pain. The quest can become an obsession to get hold of that one thing that will (supposedly) finally eliminate the deep-rooted feeling of not having enough or not being enough. It will never work, until Christ truly becomes the satisfaction of your soul.

Whether the cause is simple greed or something more complex, the truth remains that wolves live to get, never to give.

It is obvious what kind of life develops out of trying to get your own way all the time: repetitive, loveless, cheap sex; a stinking accumulation of mental and emotional garbage; frenzied and joyless grabs for happiness; trinket gods; magic-show religion; paranoid loneliness; cutthroat competition; all-consuming-yet-never-satisfied wants; a brutal temper; an impotence to love or be loved; divided homes and divided lives; small-minded and lopsided pursuits; the vicious habit of depersonalizing everyone into a rival; uncontrolled and uncontrollable addictions; ugly parodies of community. I could go on.

This isn't the first time I have warned you, you know. If you use your freedom this way, you will not inherit God's kingdom.

But what happens when we live God's way? He brings gifts into our lives, much the same way that fruit appears in an orchard—things like affection for others, exuberance about life, serenity. We develop

a willingness to stick with things, a sense of compassion in the heart, and a conviction that a basic
holiness permeates things and people. We find ourselves involved in loyal commitments, not needing
to force our way in life, able to marshal and direct
our energies wisely. (Gal. 5:19–23 THE MESSAGE)

We are called to spread the aroma of Christ in our world. This
will require a totally different, you might even call it an *unnatural,*
way of dealing with life. We cannot feed our "normal" but fleshly
desires of pride, power, and prejudice if we want to achieve this godly
outcome.

Some people who are governed by greed come to Jesus in hopes
of being blessed financially in a radical way. Many Christians have
unknowingly embraced an erroneous theological premise, thinking
that proclaiming the promises and exercising their so-called faith
guarantees a life of financial prosperity. Or at the least, they believe
that their faith-filled engagement will cause God to change their
circumstances to their benefit. This is many times wolf motivation
with a spiritual cloak.

To them, God becomes the dispenser of blessings and the one
who will supply more of what they want and desire to live a more opu-
lent and comfortable life. They believe their diligence in doing things
right is what will secure their hoped-for breakthroughs and this will
be the guarantee of the so-called blessings. It involves a quid-pro-quo
arrangement with God. If you do what you should, then you get what
you desire from God, who rewards good behavior. Indeed, sometimes
we even call this a blessing, though it feeds fleshly greed and ego.

Goats and Sheep

The other kind of taker, in Jesus's book, is goats. Unlike wolves, whose greed causes them to want to take from others, goats are self-centered people whose motto is "What's mine is mine, and I'm going to keep it."

Goats pride themselves that they are not wolves. They might not be greedy, but they most definitely are selfish. These people lack consideration for others. They are concerned chiefly with their own profit and pleasure. They are preoccupied with themselves and their own affairs. Their focus on their own self-interest is so great that the well-being of others is of little importance.

Jesus taught that a time was coming when all mankind would be separated into two groups, which He metaphorically referred to as sheep and goats. The goats were those who focused solely on their own desires, needs, and interests and did not reach out to people in need. The sheep, on the other hand, are generous with their time, resources, and love.

> When the Son of Man comes in His glory, and all the holy angels with Him, then He will sit on the throne of His glory. All the nations will be gathered before Him, and He will separate them one from another, as a shepherd divides his sheep from the goats. And He will set the *sheep* on His right hand, but the *goats* on the left. Then the King will say to those on His right hand, "Come, you blessed of My Father, inherit the kingdom prepared for you

from the foundation of the world: for I was hungry and you gave Me food; I was thirsty and you gave Me drink; I was a stranger and you took Me in; I was naked and you clothed Me; I was sick and you visited Me; I was in prison and you came to Me."

Then the righteous will answer Him, saying, "Lord, when did we see You hungry and feed You, or thirsty and give You drink? When did we see You a stranger and take You in, or naked and clothe You? Or when did we see You sick, or in prison, and come to You?" And the King will answer and say to them, "Assuredly, I say to you, *inasmuch as you did it to one of the least of these My brethren, you did it to Me.*" (Matt. 25:31–40)

I must admit, this is one of those passages in Scripture that scares me. Jesus says that we will be evaluated in the future based on how we treat people in the here and now. I don't understand this completely, except to say that Jesus clearly expects us to live unselfish lives and bless those around us.

Jesus calls people sheep, in a very good sense, when they live generous lives. These people are a wellspring of kindness, bringing life-giving encouragement and affirmation to others. They choose to offer their time, skills, and resources to serve others in ways that reflect the very generosity that God showed when Christ became human.

We don't become this kind of sheep through a one-off outreach engagement. It's a way of posturing your whole life. It is a mind-set that now governs the way you approach the world around you.

Let this *mind be in you* which was also in Christ
Jesus, who, being in the form of God, did not consider it robbery to be equal with God, but *made
Himself* of no reputation, taking the form of a bond-
servant, and coming in the likeness of men. And
being found in appearance as a man, He humbled
Himself and became obedient to the point of death,
even the death of the cross. (Phil. 2:5–8)

Sheep live with an abundance mentality, not a scarcity mentality.
Sheep are convinced that God is the source of all they have, and they
live to bless and serve those around them. These are the people who
truly spread the aroma of Christ within a community.

Sheep in the Workplace

What of "sheep" in the world of business or commerce? Christ followers sometimes struggle to integrate Christianity into their everyday
lives in the workplace. There is a feeling among some believers that
business ethics and Christian convictions are so far different as to be
irreconcilable.

Many business situations encourage cutthroat competition and
backstabbing betrayals. People throw others under the bus to get
ahead. Christian character traits such as generosity, love, compassion, forgiveness, integrity, and contentment seem like the qualities
of the person who doesn't get the promotion.

But wait a minute! If Christianity isn't suitable for the workplace,
where is it suitable? If Christian character doesn't work in the office

or classroom or construction site, where does it work? If biblical ethics aren't relevant for the marketplace, then they are not relevant for any area of our lives.

The truth is that anti-Christian or fleshly behavior may indeed get a person ahead in the short run. But the betrayer will be betrayed, the cheater will be found out, and the unethical will be exposed.

Still, it's not rare for Christians to have trouble adjusting to the new way of living. They might have learned how to play the game as non-Christians, so, when they come to the office as new believers, the old habits might kick in. It will take a while to make that transition from living according to the old rules to living according to the new. This is why the concept of identity is so central to the new life in Christ. As already communicated in earlier chapters, identity precedes activity.

For some Christ followers, this seems far to go from a consumer-driven, self-centered life to a life of generosity and self-sacrifice. Sometimes they start with something that feels generous but really is not. Perhaps they measure what they have to give, be it time or resources, and give out of their abundance. But creaming off the top is hardly a sacrificial engagement.

Once again, I am not suggesting that we should shy away from affluence and abundance. But there will be times when we will be challenged to give beyond what is comfortable, and that's when true generosity will be tested.

Life-giving generosity happens when we abandon ourselves to serve others. It's a countercultural and counterintuitive progression from

- Wolves—being greedy and materialistically driven, to
- Goats—being self-centered, to
- Sheep—becoming stewards of what God has entrusted to us, to
- Lambs—becoming fully generous people.

Being a good steward is admirable. We are all stewards or managers of those things entrusted to us, inherited by us, and earned by us. We are stewards of our wealth, our possessions, our families, our time, our gifts and talents, our physical bodies, our souls, and our spiritual journeys. But we should aim for a deep, inward transformation from mere stewards to spontaneous, generous givers. Because "God loves a cheerful giver" (2 Cor. 9:7).

Generosity is beyond stewardship, which is taking a posture of responsible earning, managing, and giving. Generosity is more organic, more life-giving, and less legalistic and formal than stewardship. Generosity is evaluated based on the amount of cheerfulness behind it. Giving grudgingly or out of obligation is not generosity.

Lambs

To become generous, you must give. Generosity grows through the action of sharing and giving away. This might be what Jesus had in mind when He sent His disciples out as lambs:

> Go your way; behold, I send you out as lambs among wolves. (Luke 10:3)

Can you feel the tension in this statement? It seems implied that they would feel vulnerable. But this is the kingdom life that we exhibit. I'm sure this is what Paul meant when he said, "When I am weak, then I am strong" (2 Cor. 12:10).

Lambs, it seems, are unintimidated by whether they have much or little. Lambs know they are empowered by God and His miraculous provision.

The disciples did go out as lambs among wolves, carrying neither money nor backpack, yet they had remarkable success and came back to Jesus with great joy (see Luke 10).

Evidently, they discovered that living in deep dependency and extravagant generosity is something God richly rewards.

> In that hour Jesus rejoiced in the Spirit and said, "I thank You, Father, Lord of heaven and earth, that You have hidden these things from the wise and prudent and revealed them to babes." (Luke 10:21)

There is something glorious about finally understanding the generosity paradigm. It challenges the deepest presuppositions driving our culture, which is full of wolves and goats. Yet the highest joy comes to sheep and lambs.

Could we become the generation in which Christians become known as givers? Could we be the community that practices the art of serving and blessing the people around us? If we could, it might well prove to be more profound than every other program and strategy we have ever used in our efforts to transform Babylon.

Generosity in South Florida

Many people—even many Christians—live only to make a good impression on others or please themselves. But selfishness always brings discord. This is why Paul stressed spiritual unity:

> Make me truly happy by agreeing wholeheartedly with each other, loving one another, and working together with one mind and purpose.
>
> Don't be selfish; don't try to impress others. Be humble, thinking of others as better than yourselves. Don't look out only for your own interests, but take an interest in others, too.
>
> You must have the same attitude that Christ Jesus had. (Phil. 2:2–5 NLT)

Don't be so concerned about making a good impression or meeting your own needs that you strain relationships in God's family. There is something amazing that happens when generosity is expressed through corporate unity in the body of Christ. When we work together, caring for the problems of others as if they were our problems, we demonstrate Christ's example of putting others first, exhibiting generosity, and demonstrating unity.

I have been blessed to witness an amazing unity movement rising up among churches in the South Florida region. The leaders of these churches came together and made a commitment to reach out to Broward County as the collective church, and now they are united under the banner of Church United and LSF (Love South Florida).

Originally their commitment was to seek opportunities to tangibly bless the community only during the month of November 2016.

Here is the article, written by Edwin Copeland, that was published in the *Good News Florida* newspaper on January 3, 2017:

> Church United, a collaborative movement with over 50 churches from various denominations committed to mobilizing the Church to serve South Florida, spent the entire month of November successfully executing an initiative called "Love South Florida." Congregants of participating churches were challenged to "Love, Give + Serve" in support of this never before seen outreach to demonstrate the Love of God all across our region.
>
> Kicking off the weekend of October 29, congregations were challenged to LOVE by participating in random acts of kindness—paying it forward in a drive through, inviting a new neighbor over for dinner, and then to share their efforts on social media using #LOVESFL. November 5 began a two-week focus on GIVE as churches responded to tangible community needs by collectively donating food and money to people and organizations in need. The final week of November 26 congregants were challenged to SERVE by giving of themselves and their time to benefit a local community organization.
>
> In total, Love South Florida raised over $200,000 for organizations and projects seeking to

make Broward county a better place to live, work and raise a family. An additional 50,000 pounds of food was donated to local food pantries and over 20,000 hours of community service were logged.

At the end of the day, Love South Florida was an outward expression of the vision of Church United—a movement to see the Churches of our community come together to connect, collaborate and celebrate with one another. Driven by the simple guiding principle that no one single denomination or key leader is going to bring about tangible change to this region, Church United believes that we are all stronger together. To them, the Love South Florida initiative was only the beginning.[13]

Leaders from churches and denominations across South Florida now work right alongside other pastors, leaders, and churches. It's marvelous. Churches are working together to provide crisis housing for single mothers and children and to share meals with the homeless. They're working together to care for modern-day orphans and widows, providing love and generosity toward "the least of these my brothers" (Matt. 25:40 ESV), the lost and the marginalized in our community. They're being sheep, not goats, to the people of South Florida.

We're now seeing churches asking questions of their neighbors and local schools, questions no one else was asking, and providing innovative solutions. Just as courageous soldiers "run to the guns" to keep others safe, these churches are running toward the brokenness of their communities, bringing beauty from ashes.

It is beautiful when God's people set aside their denominational and ecclesiastical differences and live simply as citizens of a new kingdom. When that happens, powerful solutions to complex problems emerge, unimaginable resources are discovered, and Christ's kingdom advances.

Generosity in the Face of Tragedy

On January 6, 2017, Esteban Santiago allegedly went on a shooting spree at the Fort Lauderdale airport. Panic swept the South Florida airport, and in the end, five people were dead and six others wounded.

In the midst of the world's shock over this horrible attack, Church United sensed this as an opportunity to show the love of Christ in the face of hate.

We immediately asked how the church could serve the community in this crisis. We were able to serve food and water to stranded passengers, affected families, and the media. But people's lives had ended that day, and we wanted to press further into this need.

In coordination with the Broward County Health Department and the FBI's assistance advocates, Church United rallied the Broward County churches to pay for the medical expenses of all those directly affected by the shooting. We needed to raise $31,000 to cover the immediate expenses, but those twenty-plus churches went above and beyond to meet this need. They raised $56,000 in cash and an additional $3,000 in gift cards to benefit the families who were temporarily displaced.

The thing that left me speechless was that, had God not brought about the rise of Church United in the months preceding the tragedy, that incredible response may never have happened, and the glory that came to God out of our response would never have come. All these churches mobilized a response within twenty-four hours of the event—all because the organization was already in place, even if the paint wasn't dry on the walls, so to speak. It almost seemed that Church United—and perhaps unity movements across the world—had been raised up for just such a time as this.

Unity for unity's sake won't change the spiritual, cultural, and social temperature of a community. However, unity for the sake of the kingdom can.

As the church continues to be divinely connected, one with another, fresh opportunities to engage the lostness, pain, and brokenness of any region will arise. The world doesn't seem to be trending toward fewer needs for movements like Church United. Quite the opposite, actually.

Love South Florida was a small example of what can happen when God's people collaborate. What's so exciting is that we believe we're just getting started. It's incredible to imagine what can still be achieved through this expression of unity and mission of generosity toward this region.

What if God's people work together to raise the number of generous Christians in our community? What if we work together to see broken families renewed and lives restored? What if we invest together in increasing the quality of marriages and families? Might it slow the divorce rate? Might those families become units of generosity in the community? What if we were to invest in transforming local schools and educational institutions, turning failing schools around and raising the literacy level of the region?

Imagine what *your* region could look like if the churches came together, living out of this generous life, giving, serving, and blessing your community. Imagine Babylon transformed!

13

GOING TO THE "OTHER SIDE"

We live in Babylon. I think we've established that pretty well by this point. This is Babylon, not Jerusalem. It's a broken, fallen world, not the garden of Eden. And while the kingdom of God may be among us, no one would say that God's will is done on Earth to the degree that it is done in heaven. The culture around us does not align itself with the Christian worldview, much less to Christian forms of behavior.

Because of this, many Christ followers feel we need to band together and isolate ourselves from this hostile environment. If we're under siege, then by all means we need to build a castle, go inside, and pull up the drawbridge.

If we do that, we may indeed feel safer, but we will also become an obscure subculture that has lost connection with society. The hermit living in seclusion can't complain that he has no impact on the society he's turned his back on.

So how can we drop the drawbridge, raise the portcullis, and reengage society? How can we cause the surrounding community to desire more of Christ, without presenting the gospel message in a way they will reject? I'm not talking only about social action in the world. I'm talking about engaging people so they can discover Jesus Christ. We serve and love and engage, and by doing so, we cause others to hunger for Christ.

The Keys to Babylon

Christians are often surprised to discover they already hold the keys to Babylon. Christ followers burdened by the lostness, pain, and brokenness of their communities are wonderfully equipped to engage this hostile, self-centered, self-serving Babylonian environment.

Service

The first key is service. When we start to serve our communities, we have a far greater connection to its people than when we come out proclaiming the good news only. You have to earn the right to speak to people, especially if you're asking them to change their lives. Who are they more likely to listen to: the person who has been hip-deep with them in the work of building and restoring a neighborhood or the stranger who swoops in with some gospel tracts? Serve first, and share your faith second. Jesus first engaged with grace, and then He shared the truth.

Doxa Deo has an inner-city campus in the heart of downtown Pretoria. Years ago, the youth group there wanted to go clean the train station. Because the station was city property, they had to get permission first. They made an appointment with the appropriate councilor and asked her permission to clean the station. At first, she was wary about young people wanting to clean something free of charge. She wanted to know where they came from and who had sent them to volunteer for this. When they said they were from our church, she sat back and exclaimed, "Doxa Deo *again?*"

To me, that is one of the most beautiful testimonies of our ministry: "Doxa Deo again."

That councilor went on to become the mayor of our city and, as you might guess, one of our biggest allies. She also became a patron of our POPUP skills development program.

By serving your city, you will come to understand and alleviate the hurts and needs in the hostile culture of Babylon around you. And when you do that, opportunities will open up to bring salvation to its citizens.

Wisdom

The second key is wisdom. The institutions of our world are running out of answers for the complexities of today. But Christians are led by the Holy Spirit, and He's never out of ideas. We can rely on Him to give us wisdom and solutions when worldly wisdom dries up.

When we become engaged in all spheres of society, we will find ourselves in situations in which decisions must be made for the community. Christians bring to the table a higher wisdom, one that is sensible, intelligent, and serves the greater good. Godly wisdom shows a path forward that is not swayed by consumerism or personal interest and is free of the culture's usual disregard for the welfare of others. *Wisdom* may be best defined as "that good judgment which uses knowledge appropriately for a beneficial outcome." As our lives become aligned with the fundamental principles of Scripture and we learn to live with sensitivity to the leading of the Holy Spirit, we develop as the ambassadors of the kingdom, who will be known for the wisdom we bring to challenging situations.

In 1994, when we first got this vision to embrace our city, many changes in South African society were taking place. The largest was that the policy of apartheid gave way to a whole new democratic order. For this, most of the people in the country were deeply grateful. By the way, the church played a mammoth role in the facilitation of this transition. However, not all the changes were positive. The new government stipulated that every major city in South Africa should build a casino. This was a way for the new government to raise money, so it made sense from that perspective.

But the spiritual leaders in the city didn't want a casino in Pretoria. We were acutely aware of the economic disparities in our region, and we knew the effect that the lure of easy money would have on those who were already in dire financial straits. As far as we were concerned, this was injustice to our society.

We wanted to fight it, but we knew we couldn't just tell the government we didn't want a casino. That wouldn't work. We realized we had to clarify *why* we didn't want it in our city. So we began researching the social impact a casino has on a community. Mostly, we prayed for wisdom about how to approach this challenge.

There was a man in our church who served on the city council. We felt he would be the key to get this dialogue on the city agenda.

He agreed to take our concerns to the council, so when he stood before them to speak, we prayed for him to receive divine favor and wisdom—and the favor of the council. The council heard his statement and asked him to present a report about casino impact at their next meeting.

We rejoiced at that outcome. He presented the research at the next meeting, and the council decided to withdraw their intent to build the casino. What a turnaround! And he did it without quoting one scripture or invoking Jesus's name (though of course there was much prayer flowing all around). He merely engaged with wisdom and was able to serve the well-being of the city.

This is how you can serve your community too. At that point, our city was the only one in South Africa that did not get a casino. It took one man serving with wisdom! We must pray that God gives us moments when the wisdom that comes from above can improve the destiny of a community.

Power

The third key to Babylon is power. When God rolls up His sleeves and shows His might, people can't help but stop and take notice.

We know God wants to do miraculous things in our communities. And just one moment of the power of God changes everything. We need to anticipate these divine moments. When people are amazed at what is happening, they ask new questions.

> You shall receive power when the Holy Spirit has
> come upon you; and you shall be witnesses to Me

in Jerusalem, and in all Judea and Samaria, and to
the end of the earth. (Acts 1:8)

Some would say that this prophecy was given to the eleven
apostles and did not apply to anyone beyond them or any time
beyond then. But I believe it continues and applies to all Christians
on through to today. For one, the gospel was not taken to the ends
of the earth before the Eleven had all passed away. For another, Acts
records stories of people other than the apostles receiving power from
the Spirit.

The power to be Jesus's witnesses continues to be ours. Miracles,
especially those that are designed to spread the word and witness
about Christ, persist to today. I've seen them.

But if that's true, why is it that we do not see God performing
miracles in many parts of the world? If power is a key to transforming Babylon, why are miracles so few and far between?

I believe it is because Christians don't trust God for miracles or
they have been deceived into believing that God doesn't want to do
miracles where they are. In Jesus's day, there are signs that His power
was in a sense limited, perhaps self-limited, in places where people
didn't believe in Him (see Matt. 13:58). It seems to be a principle
that the miraculous power of God is unlikely to show itself in places,
or people, where there is little expectation of divine engagement.

God is performing miracles today. His power is flowing across
the earth. Pray for Him to perform miracles in your community, as
this will open doors to transformation.

God gives us the keys to step into previously unreachable environments for the sake of the kingdom. Instead of trying to escape

Babylon, we can now turn our faces toward it with the intent to boldly engage it.

The Value of Humanity

Most of us prefer to stick with the known and comfortable. We like our people and our stomping grounds and our favorite shops and our neighborhoods. It can be quite easy to somehow never find a need to go to the other side of town. Or the other side of the state, or the country, or the world.

We can begin to think of "our people" as the only ones worth talking to and the only ones worthy of trust. People from the other side of the tracks or across the aisle or in another tax bracket are different, by which we almost mean *inferior* or *unclean*.

Yet Scripture reminds us that every person matters to the Maker. He is mindful of each one of us.

> Before I formed you in the womb I knew you;
> Before you were born I sanctified you. (Jer. 1:5)

In the garden of Eden, Adam and Eve broke God's only law, and the world was cast into a fallen state because of it. Mankind entered into a broken, *lost* situation, and in some ways, we're still in that state.

But lost doesn't mean forgotten. Nor does it mean abandoned.

In a sense, the Devil stole mankind from God, at least temporarily. The serpent deceived Eve in the garden, and God had to cast away the pinnacle and point of His creation. But while a thief may hold onto stolen goods for a while, he is never the rightful owner. A thief never takes ownership. To this day, mankind remains the property of God.

In Adam, we all fell away from God. But in Christ, God erased that separation. The cross dealt with every reason mankind could have to feel separated from God. Jesus is the highway in the desert:

> The voice of one crying in the wilderness:
> "Prepare the way of the LORD;
> Make straight in the desert
> A highway for our God.
> Every valley shall be exalted
> And every mountain and hill brought low;
> The crooked places shall be made straight
> And the rough places smooth;
> The glory of the LORD shall be revealed,
> And all flesh shall see it together;
> For the mouth of the LORD has spoken."
> (Isa. 40:3–5)

All mankind belongs to God. He desires that everyone be saved and come to the knowledge of the truth (see 1 Tim. 2:4).

When we look at the citizens of Babylon around us, we must see them as precious subjects of the same King we serve. They may look or smell or dress different, and they may come from the "other side," but they are beloved by God. Just as you and I were beloved by Him even before we were citizens of the kingdom.

Christ is the bread of life to every human being, not just to those who are already saved and in church. The gospel story reveals God's love not only for us but also for others.

Going to the Other Side

When Jesus walked the earth in human form, many of the people who heard Him teach had a hard time with this concept. The Jews had believed for centuries that they were special to God. Sure, all people were special to Him, but they were the *most* special. The elite. The only ones who worshipped Him and held His Law and called on His name.

The corollary to that was that everyone who wasn't Jewish wasn't special. Not *as* special. Not on the inside. Not privileged to the goodness of God, and certainly not candidates for any sort of afterlife with Him (with a few very rare exceptions).

Anyone from the other side of the river was out. Anyone from the other side of the boundary line was out. Anyone from the other side of the sea or the continent or the world was out. Anyone from any other religion was way out.

By the time of Jesus's ministry, they had become so insular and so good at drawing narrow circles around themselves that even certain Jews had become "out." If you worked in certain jobs, you were out, even if you were Jewish. If you talked to certain people, you were out. If you broke certain rules, you were out. If you sinned, you were out. In the end, all you had to do was make one of the Jewish religious leaders mad, and you'd be put out and excluded (see John 9:34).

Jesus stepped into an arena that was obsessed with turning people into outsiders, yet He Himself was all about bringing people back in. Humanity excludes, shuns, and condemns. But God rescues, includes, and restores.

Whereas all the Jews wanted to stay on *this* side of things, on the correct side of restrictions and boundaries and behaviors, Jesus said, "Let us cross over to the other side" (Mark 4:35).

Sometimes when He said this, He only meant back to the town they used as their home base or over to some other "good" Jewish town. But this time, He meant something else, and the disciples didn't want to do it.

Because the spot on the other side of the Sea of Galilee He was referring to this time was the *wrong* side. It was the heathen side, the pig-eating side. It was where "the nations" (aka the Gentiles) lived. There probably wasn't a Jew alive at that time who would've thought it a good idea to go to *that* other side.

Besides, if they went to the other side, they would become ceremonially unclean, and they'd have to go through a whole cleansing ceremony when they came back. How much easier just to remain on this side and stay clean.

They didn't understand why Jesus wanted them to go to the other side, and they definitely didn't want to do it, but since it was Jesus commanding them to go, they piled into the boat and started rowing. About halfway through the journey, Jesus lay down in the boat and went to sleep! I secretly wonder whether He was testing them. Without His eye on them, I'm sure they were tempted to turn the boat around and claim they'd gotten lost or something.

So there they were in the middle of a big lake, and the wind began to pick up—a storm was brewing. The sea must've become very rough indeed, because these seasoned fishermen became anxious. They'd seen a storm or two in their lives, and this one was different. I suspect they remembered superstitions that going to the non-Jewish side of the lake would bring a curse, yet that was where they were steadily rowing toward.

Is it any wonder they woke Jesus up? "Teacher, do You not care that we are perishing?" (Mark 4:38). I think they were actually saying, "Why are You doing this to us?"

Why are You taking us over to the other side?

As if He'd been waiting for their touch, Jesus hopped up and spoke to the storm, calming it with His word. I'm sure the disciples looked at one another absolutely amazed. "Who can this be, that even the wind and the sea obey Him!" (Mark 4:41).

When they reached the other side, the region called the Decapolis, there was no welcoming committee or girls approaching to put flower leis around their necks. The people on the other side didn't want anything to do with the Jews, who considered them filthy and subhuman, any more than the Jews wanted anything to do with them.

They pulled up next to a cemetery, and out popped a demon-possessed madman. I can picture the disciples thinking, "Great! There's nobody here but demoniacs. First a spooky storm and now a guy full of demons! I told you we should've stayed home."

But instead of getting back into the boat, Jesus strode toward the madman, almost as if to say, "Yep, this is our man. This is why we came to the other side."

Jesus drove the many demons out of the man, and those spirits jumped into a large herd of pigs nearby—and then those pigs went insane, committing mass suicide by jumping off a cliff into the sea.

The disciples didn't want to be there. The demons hadn't wanted Jesus to be there. Then the people of the "other side" came out, having realized that the death of the pig herd instantly decimated their livelihoods, and now *they* didn't want Jesus there. About the only one glad to have Jesus around was the man from whom a legion of demons had passed out.

Everyone begged Jesus to leave, so He turned to get into the boat. But the former demon-possessed man clung to Him, pleading to go with Him wherever He would go.

However, Jesus wouldn't let him. Jesus was so smart: He knew He had just found the key to the whole region. This man had just become the key to reaching the entire region of the "other side." Those people wouldn't listen to Jesus if He strode ashore and tried to preach. Why should they? He was a Jew, after all. But they would listen to one of their own, one for whom Christ had done an incredible work. Jesus told him,

> Go home to your friends, and tell them what
> great things the Lord has done for you, and how
> He has had compassion on you. (Mark 5:19)

And listen to what happened in that whole country as a result of Jesus going to the other side:

He departed and began to proclaim in Decapolis
all that Jesus had done for him; and all marveled.
(Mark 5:20)

On top of everything else, these words to the former demoniac must've flustered the disciples even further. When they were in Israel, the land of the Jews, Jesus often followed His miracles with a stern instruction for the healed person *not* to tell anyone what had happened. But here, on the other side, He told the man to go out and tell everyone.

What was going *on* that day? Jesus was teaching them that God cares for every human being, not just those like us but also all those on the other side.

I'm sure the disciples were happy to get back to the Israel side. "Thank God we're back!" Maybe Peter knelt down and kissed the sand.

Very soon things went back to normal. Miracles began happening again, and then they fed five thousand people. Can you imagine how excited they would've been? I mean, they were on the crest of the wave—they just experienced a miracle happening through their own hands.

How awful it must've sounded to them when Jesus said, "Go over to the other side" (see Matt. 14:22–33). What? Again? They probably thought they were done with those pagans. Nothing could have been a bigger downer on their jubilation and festive spirit than Jesus telling them to go over to the other side. This was the very place they'd been chased away from very recently.

And the good news just kept coming. Jesus said He wasn't going along. This was dreadful news for them, because they had to get into the boat and row over to the other side while it was getting dark. If anything bad happened to them on their way this time, a storm or anything else, Jesus would not be there to save them.

Sure enough, in the middle of the night the waves started picking up, and it became clear they were in trouble again. But Jesus did the most incredible thing—walked *on the water* to meet them. Can you blame these disciples for thinking He was a ghost? They were living with this superstition, this awareness that something should go wrong, and then someone came walking on the water.

Jesus said, "It is I; I am not a ghost," and acted as though He was going to pass them by. He did not want to get into the boat, but then Peter spoiled the program by getting out of the boat, walking, and sinking, so Jesus had to help him get back in the boat.

Then they arrived on the other side. Scholars are divided on this, but there is reason to believe that the "other side" here is again the Decapolis—right back where they'd been with the demoniac and the pigs.

This time, instead of the locals rallying against them, we see a crowd gathering soon after His arrival. Why? Because the man who had been set free from the demons had told everybody his story! Jesus knew that this man's story would create a desire in people to bring to Jesus the sick and those who were oppressed by evil to be healed and set free the next time He came to this region. Jesus had found the key to an unclean region.

This is what we believe God wants *us* to discover as we navigate Babylon: He wants to give us keys to be able to access unclean regions.

Not long after, Jesus ministered to a crowd of four thousand, and then the same thing happened: they got hungry. And then the disciples had to start dishing out bread and fish to the people again. They started with a few loaves of bread and a few fish, and the same miracle happened. But there's a difference. This time, the people receiving the bounty from God's hand were Gentiles. Non-Jews. Would God really feed people from the unclean nations of Canaan just as He'd done for the "clean" people from the twelve tribes of Israel? Once again, there was surplus after the miracle, and they picked up seven baskets full of leftovers.

When they were in the boat again, Jesus taught the disciples this lesson:

> And He left them, and getting into the boat again, departed to the other side. Now the disciples had forgotten to take bread, and they did not have more than one loaf with them in the boat. Then He charged them, saying, "Take heed, beware of the leaven of the Pharisees and the leaven of Herod."
>
> And they reasoned among themselves, saying, "It is because we have no bread."
>
> But Jesus, being aware of it, said to them, "Why do you reason because you have no bread? Do you not yet perceive nor understand? Is your heart still hardened? Having eyes, do you not see? And having ears, do you not hear? And do you not remember? When I broke the five loaves for the five

thousand, how many baskets full of fragments did you take up?"

They said to Him, "Twelve."

"Also, when I broke the seven for the four thousand, how many large baskets full of fragments did you take up?"

And they said, "Seven."

So He said to them, "How is it you do not understand?" (Mark 8:13–21)

Jesus reminded them that when they were on the Israel side, they had fed the twelve tribes of Israel and then picked up twelve baskets full of what was left over. And when they were with the seven nations of Canaan, they fed four thousand people and picked up seven baskets of leftovers. "So He said to them, 'How is it you do not understand?'" (Mark 8:21).

They didn't understand, and I didn't either! Until one day I saw it: twelve tribes, twelve baskets; seven nations, seven baskets.

In essence, Jesus was saying, "When we were feeding those two groups of people, we were not just feeding hungry people. This was a prophetic statement saying that I, as the Bread of Life, have come to feed the world. There is enough of Me to feed all Israel. But we went back to the Decapolis to say that there is enough of Me to feed the unclean side too, to feed all the heathen nations."

It's as though He was saying, "This side and that side—they're all My side!"

This is the bold proclamation: our Savior has come to all the nations of the earth, and all communities, cities, environments, and spheres of society will be fed and satisfied when they discover the true Bread of Life.

God wants us to walk the streets of Babylon. He placed us *in* Babylon and told us to seek the welfare of the city. That means leaving our ceremonially clean compounds and walking in unclean regions where people may dislike us because they think we look down on them, where people aren't similar to us, where they don't do the religious things we do and where they practice things we hate, where demons roam and entire industries exist that stand opposed to God's laws.

Because it's in Babylon that many lost, stolen sheep are and He wants them back.

May God give the church a clear understanding that we are called not only to our little side, and may we find the keys with which to touch every unreached people group and every sphere of society so that our world is transformed into a place where Christ's love truly reigns.

CONCLUSION

God loves people.

God loves cities.

Both people and cities are God's idea!

They are not inherently evil, and they are redeemable.

Global urbanization is an opportunity for God's people to be *present* with those who need what believers have. There are no fewer than eleven hundred references to cities in the Bible. Many of these references express God's love and concern for the people in those cities.

In this book, I have shown how God has revealed His compassion for our communities and how He wants to manifest that compassion through us. Understanding that God has intentionally *brought* us to these cities will change the paradigm from which we live and do ministry.

Our world is changing. The rate at which things are shifting in our world is staggering. Massive societal changes, globally and locally, seem to happen at an accelerating pace. New trends, opportunities, and rapidly developing technology define our reality. It is within this context of the constant redefinition of reality that the Christian presence is so important. More than ever, we need to be out in the classrooms, boardrooms, and marketplaces of Babylon.

The future of the church is truly on the "other side."

Christians, Jesus told us, are the salt of the earth (see Matt. 5:13). One way to understand that is to see us as little grains of Christ's presence sprinkled here and there throughout our entire culture, preserving its life, staving off its rot, and bringing delight and satisfaction to an otherwise dead and flavorless world.

The light of Christ is what our dark globe needs, and the church is God's strategy for delivering it. When Christ followers are out there in the community, engaging every sphere of society, they bring hope, vision, direction, alignment, and stability to people's lives and to society as a whole.

Jesus told His disciples that the Holy Spirit would glorify Him by taking from what was His and revealing it (see John 16:14–15). In the same way, we glorify Christ when we take from all He has given us—compassion, peace, purpose, wisdom, generosity, and every other spiritual benefit—and give it out to those around us who desperately need it. We break it apart like bits of bread and watch our Lord do miracles.

Wherever Christianity has gone, societies have been radically transformed. It always starts with spiritual transformation in the lives of people in the community, and then it inevitably results in a wake of societal impact. Cultural transformation follows authentic spiritual and social transformation in a community.

When Christianity is embraced in a culture, orphanages are started, schools and universities are formed, and hospitals are founded. The hungry are fed, the homeless are sheltered, and the sick and dying are comforted and even healed. Families are strengthened and broken relationships are restored. Society becomes humane and justice starts to flourish. People are presented with environments in which their lives can flourish.

It is clear: Jesus Christ is Lord of all reality, and if He is allowed to do so, His presence brings life and order to every sphere of society.

- He is Lord of the church.
- He is Lord of government.
- He is Lord of business.
- He is Lord of education.
- He is Lord of the arts.
- He is Lord of the media.
- He is Lord of social services.
- He is Lord of sports.

These spheres of society make sense only when they come into alignment with His lordship. They cannot function to their full potential if they are not transformed by God.

If this is true, Christianity has something to say about all those spheres of society. It is within this context that we need to grapple with our sense of mission and our calling as the church.

Unfortunately, we have sometimes contributed to a dualistic separation mentality. We have created a certain kind of Christ follower: on Sunday he can seem to be a spiritual giant, but Monday through

Saturday, when he engages the real world, well, that's different. Out there, he doesn't feel he needs to even think "missionally," much less talk or behave "missionally." His faith might keep him from behaving like everyone around him—perhaps helping him not to cheat, lie, or curse—but that's about the extent of it. Somehow the church has never been able to transfer Christ's mission into his "real life." We've collapsed faith with morality, and morality kills off real life!

I personally feel this is a failure of the church, not of the person in the pew. I believe we have preached the gospel of salvation to the neglect of the gospel of the kingdom. We know that redemption has a personal salvation dimension, of course, but we miss the mission of restoring all things that was included in the redemption moment of the cross.

Jesus isn't king of our personal lives only. He is also the triumphant Lord of the earth who wants to transform every sphere of our world.

> Now thanks be to God who always leads us in triumph in Christ, and through us diffuses the fragrance of His knowledge in every place. For we are to God the fragrance of Christ among those who are being saved and among those who are perishing. To the one we are the aroma of death leading to death, and to the other the aroma of life leading to life. (2 Cor. 2:14–16)

As Christ followers, we can be the presence of Christ in our cities. We do so by

- embracing the presence of Jesus in our individual lives, especially in the context of our everyday lives;
- walking together in unity with other believers and churches as the body of Christ, which is called together to serve in our specific geographical space;
- shifting our focus from just building the church to releasing Christ's fragrance in every dimension of the world;
- making the glory of God and His kingdom the focus of everything we are and do;
- blessing our cities and seeking their peace and welfare; and
- building bridges to our communities and seeking keys to engage previously unreached areas.

Reclaiming Your Identity

If we are to effectively navigate Babylon, we must become more aware of what we represent as followers of Christ. Perhaps the most tragic consequence of the fall was the loss of humanity's understanding of our true identity. A fallen state was introduced, and humanity became subject to the authority of sin. We lived no more in a perfect garden but in an environment ruled by deterioration and decay, and the authority we found ourselves under wasn't the realm of God's blessed delight but temporal systems of corruption and selfishness.

Each of us inherited a set of damaged values and prejudices that had been passed down to us from generations going back to the fall of Adam. These cripple relationships at every level of society.

The greatest contradiction to humanity's true identity is living according to an inferior self-opinion. What kept Israel out of the Promised Land was not a lack of faith in the supernatural. After all, they'd witnessed the supernatural every day for forty years. What kept them sunk in defeat was how they saw themselves.

> The land through which we have gone as spies is a land that devours its inhabitants, and all the people whom we saw in it are men of great stature. There we saw the giants (the descendants of Anak came from the giants); and *we were like grasshoppers in our own sight, and so we were in their sight.* (Num. 13:32–33)

The way you see yourself determines the way others see you. This is a dangerous place to be if you begin to doubt the truth of your redeemed identity and innocence in Christ.

God takes pleasure in mankind. His love for us exceeds anything that could possibly disqualify humanity from entering His presence. He has broken down every reason we might have to feel distant from Him. Our reconciliation to God is the theme of the message of redemption.

Understanding our reclaimed identity is the key to transforming Babylon. The great discovery is not only that God loves us but also that He releases His love through us!

In the past, we have underestimated the gospel and its potential to affect our communities. We have concentrated on getting to heaven one day rather than on living effectively in the world around us. But Jesus came to Earth to announce the arrival of His kingdom, right then and there, and establish it in people's hearts through His death, resurrection, and ascension.

To all who believed in Him, Jesus restored their identity and citizenship rights in the kingdom of God so they could represent the presence of heaven here on Earth.

Expectancy Creates an Environment Ripe for Miracles

The moment we embrace God's promises as the basis of our expectancy, we create an environment conducive to the supernatural. If you would see the full revelation of what God has done on our behalf in Jesus Christ manifested in every dimension of our lives, you must have high expectancy.

When God speaks, it changes everything.

We see this principle in this Old Testament story of a widow who was at the end of her ability to sustain herself:

> The wife of a man from the company of the prophets cried out to Elisha, "Your servant my husband is dead, and you know that he revered the LORD. But now his creditor is coming to take my two boys as his slaves."

Elisha replied to her, "How can I help you? Tell me, what do you have in your house?"

"Your servant has nothing there at all," she said, "except a small jar of olive oil."

Elisha said, "Go around and ask all your neighbors for empty jars. Don't ask for just a few. Then go inside and shut the door behind you and your sons. Pour oil into all the jars, and as each is filled, put it to one side."

She left him and shut the door behind her and her sons. They brought the jars to her and she kept pouring. When all the jars were full, she said to her son, "Bring me another one."

But he replied, "There is not a jar left." Then the oil stopped flowing.

She went and told the man of God, and he said, "Go, sell the oil and pay your debts. You and your sons can live on what is left." (2 Kings 4:1–7 NIV)

This is not just a story of provision—it is also a story about expectancy. The prophet challenged this widow to collect as many jars as she could because he knew the oil would keep flowing according to the number of jars she collected.

When it comes to transforming the corner of Babylon God has placed you in, how many jars have you collected? What is your expectation level about what God wants to do in your life, ministry, city, and world?

May the God of hope fill you with joy and peace
in your faith, that by the power of the Holy Spirit,
your whole life and outlook may be radiant with
hope. (Rom. 15:13 PHILLIPS)

As we hear God speak over our communities and cities, we
receive His message with high expectation. His words bring into our
lives new *elevation* and new *volume*:

O Zion,
You who bring good tidings,
Get up into the high mountain;
O Jerusalem,
You who bring good tidings,
Lift up your voice with strength,
Lift it up, be not afraid;
Say to the cities of Judah, "Behold your God!"
(Isa. 40:9)

Go now, my friend, and seek the welfare of your city. Its physical
welfare, emotional welfare, and spiritual welfare. Permeate all spheres
of society with the aroma of Christ. Engage your neighbors, partner
with your fellow sojourners, and live with the expectation that God
will bring transformation. Pray for the peace and joy of the community where you have been placed. For in its welfare you find your own.

Go and be a CITY CHANGER.

NOTES

1. Rosa Flores, Mallory Simon, and Madeleine Stix, "The Disappearing Front Porch," CNN, December 1, 2016, www.cnn.com/interactive/2016/12/us /chicago-disappearing-front-porch/.

2. W. E. Vine, *Vine's Expository Dictionary of Old and New Testament Words* (Nashville: Thomas Nelson, 1997), 483.

3. "Strong's G514 - *axios*," Blue Letter Bible, accessed May 26, 2017, www.blueletterbible.org/lang/lexicon/lexicon.cfm?t=kjv&strongs=g514.

4. G. F. Handel, "XLIV. Chorus," in *The Messiah*, ed. T. Tertius Noble (New York: G. Schirmer, 1912), viii.

5. Landa Cope, "What's Wrong with This Picture?," chap. 1 in *An Introduction to the Old Testament Template: Rediscovering God's Principles for Discipling Nations* (Seattle: YWAM, 2014).

6. "Reformers in Criminal Justice," Quakers in the World, accessed May 29, 2017, www.quakersintheworld.org/quakers-in-action/43/Reformers-in-Criminal -Justice.

7. Bill Polson, "The Impact of Methodism on the Industrial Revolution in England," UMass Dartmouth, 2006, www1.umassd.edu/ir/papers/2006 /polson-william.doc.

8. Mario Lange, email message to author, April 18, 2017. Used with permission.

9. Anna Sutherland and W. Bradford Wilcox, "How Strong Families Help Create Prosperous States," Institute for Family Studies, October 21, 2015, https://ifstudies.org/blog/how-strong-families-help-create-prosperous-states.

10. Irenaeus, quoted in John Eldredge, *Waking the Dead: The Glory of a Heart Fully Alive* (Nashville: Thomas Nelson, 2003), 10.

11. Lesley Sutton, email message to author, January 29, 2017. Used with permission. Also see www.passionart.guide and www.passionart.co.uk.

12. Risco Balenke, email message to author, February 23, 2017. Used with permission.

13. Edwin Copeland, "Love SFL Impacted the Community in a Big Way," *Good News Florida*, January 3, 2017, http://goodnewsfl.org/love-south-florida -impacted-community-big-way. Used by permission of goodnewsfl.org.